MW01519185

Classroom Connections

Marilyn Doyle

PublishAmerica
Baltimore

First printing

ISBN: 1-60474-517-7
PUBLISHED BY PUBLISHAMERICA, LLLP
www.publishamerica.com
Baltimore

Printed in the United States of America

To
Robert and Tracey

INTRODUCTION

The events in the diary are accurate portrayals of actual incidents that took place over 30 years not just in the single year that is specified. Naturally, not all teaching days are as eventful as indicated. In fact, most days are rather routine and dull. However, these incidents are examples of what can and does occur in our schools on a regular basis.

SEPTEMBER

Wednesday, Sept 6

As a substitute teacher I am sure that, if I have not seen it all, I have seen most of it. From the grade primary child crying and clinging to her mother's hand to the graduate in top hat and tails, I have been there as a witness. To be sure, my career has not been all positive. Indeed there have been many negative moments, but most of the time I have had fun. I have visited and learned about different types of schools. I have been introduced to children at all age groups. I have been able to study the curriculum in all subjects and at all grade levels. I have been educated!

The pay is not the important part of substituting, but as a part-time job, substituting is among the best. I have been able to work almost every day but at the same time be at home when my children returned from school. I have had numerous experiences and met many wonderful people, most of whom were under the age of twenty. The purpose of this diary was to keep in touch with all my adventures.

Before the first day of school, I moped around the house because I didn't have a job to go to. Soon I would have to call and visit the local schools and speak to the vice-principal or head teacher in charge of substitutes, but, before I could, suddenly the phone rang. When I answered, I realized that the cycle had begun.

Already a replacement was needed. "Hello, Marilyn, can you come in tomorrow?"

"Certainly," I replied, hoping that my voice concealed my thoughts, *Hooray, hooray, I am working again. I don't have to make calls, I'm working. The money is going to start coming in again. It has been a long and poor summer.*

"I'll see you at 8:00 then," the voice went on.

"OK, where am I going?"

"Kennedy High School, math," was the answer. "See you tomorrow. Ask for John Anderson."

"Thank you," I said and hung up the phone. I hoped my voice was professional. I was elated, exalted and excited. I started jumping up and down while my cat looked askance at me. "I'm working. I'm working!"

Thursday, Sept 7

The start of a new year is always hectic. There are new parents to call, new students to meet, and new programmes to learn. If you are starting at a new school there are the additional requirements of learning the personality of the school because, just as everyone has distinct traits, so does every class and every school. All has to be done during the last week before the beginning of classes. Of course, there isn't enough time to do one of these things. Something is always left undone.

I arrived at Kennedy at 8:00 and spoke to the secretary. There was no sign of Mr. Anderson but I was told that he'll be here soon.

By 8:10 I was getting a little nervous. There was no sign of a substitute lesson plan. Where was Mr. Anderson? Where was my class? What was the schedule? Did the students come to class today? What kind of math would I be teaching?

Mr. Anderson arrived at 8:15 and showed me to my room. There was nothing there except empty desks and an empty board.

There were no books, no papers and nothing in the drawers. There were no materials of any kind, not even a student list.

I asked, "Do classes start right away?" I was hoping there would be an assembly to welcome the students.

No such luck.

"Yes," replied Mr. Anderson.

"What is my schedule?" I asked, trying not to betray my sense of panic. "What time does class start? Do I have a class list? What subjects am I teaching?"

"I'll be back," said Mr. Anderson. "Oh, by the way, classes start at 8:30 and the students will come straight to class."

I had only 15 minutes to prepare everything that is required for the first day of school and the first encounter with a class. I was still not panicking but it was getting close. What was I going to do on the first day of school? I didn't attend the orientation session. I didn't know the bell times. How long was each class? How many students do I have? What will I do for eighty minutes? I don't know what grades I am teaching. I don't know my schedule. There are no books—no papers—just me.

I sat down and thought. *OK, now I have ten minutes to plan. What will I do for the next eighty? Well, let's see. I can get their names. That'll take ten minutes. I will ask about their favourite things, summer plans and so on. That should take about another twenty minutes. I can play a name game to get to know the students. OK, that's another twenty minutes. Perhaps I'll do some math review. If only I knew what level I was teaching.*

Mr. Anderson walked in to the class at 8:25. "Here is the schedule. You'll probably be here for about two weeks. You will be teaching basic math eleven, academic math twelve and pre-calculus."

I looked at the schedule. Pre-calculus is first. PANIC! PANIC!

I had not taught grade twelve math in its entirety before. The last time I did calculus was in university, fifteen years ago.

Marilyn, I tell myself, you did it once, you can do it again. At that point, the bell rang and Mr. Anderson left. As he was leaving, I asked him to get me some materials and books.

In trooped the students. As seniors often do, they appeared a bit cocky. "We're in our final year of school," their attitude screamed. "You're new. We have been here for two years. We know more than you. We're smart. We will eat you for breakfast."

Well, no, I thought, *they won't. They may not have had breakfast but their breakfast won't be me. I, too, am smart. I am older. I will survive! I hope.*

I didn't put them in a seating plan. After all, they were in the final year of public school. They knew the rules of a class. Mr. Anderson had told me that this was a good school and a seating plan wouldn't be necessary. Of course, all the boys gravitated to the back.

There were thirty-five students in a classroom that should only hold about twenty-five. Even sitting in pairs, there was barely enough room to walk to the back of the class. I resolved to lose weight.

I started my lesson, the one I had scribbled only ten minutes before. I wasn't prepared and the students sensed it. Already they were whispering, wondering what I was going to be like. Finally, I learned their names, not by their faces but by where they were sitting. I made a seating plan for myself so I'd remember the names.

Mr. Anderson poked his head around the door. "Everything OK?" he asked.

"Fine," I replied, with no panic in my voice. "We're playing a name game."

Glen, a student, said, "Mrs. Doyle is learning our names. We don't need to because we already know each other." Everyone laughed and I joined in. So much for the name game.

Mr. Anderson dropped off some text books which I passed

out. That took about ten minutes and there was still thirty minutes to go.

No time like the present, I thought, opening the pre-calculus textbook, *might as well start.* So I turned to the first page and began. I am good actor and they didn't know that this was the first time I had looked at the page. I went over the first few examples and the bell rang. I survived Act 1—barely.

Friday, Sept 8

All children are naturally curious. They want their independence but at the same time they want rules and structure. It's much easier to tell their peers that they can't do a certain thing because they aren't allowed, than to say they won't do it because they don't want to. When they meet an adult in authority, the first step is to test. How much independence will that person allow me? What are the rules?

I arrived at Kennedy High in plenty of time to start teaching. I was fully prepared because I had stayed late the night before to get caught up and be a day ahead in my lesson plans. I was ready.

So were the students.

I couldn't walk around the classroom because of the number of students. No matter where I stood in the class, I couldn't see all the children and some of them couldn't see me.

The boys at the back of the grade twelve pre-calculus class had already started to use the class as social time. Their attitude showed that they thought they were the best students ever. After all, they were going to university next fall and they were now doing a university course. Indeed they were academically smart, but academics isn't all there is in life.

The same was true of the grade twelve class. There were some intelligent students in that class as well but most of them weren't in their senior year. They took grade ten and eleven math in their freshman year and were well on their way to becoming mathematicians, doctors, engineers or scientists.

My favourite class was the basic grade eleven class. There were only fifteen of them and they were not math students. They hated math. They had to take this class since they couldn't graduate without it. They were all struggling but they worked hard.

Many of the students in the large classes were rude. They had to be reminded to ask permission to leave the class. Telling me, "I'm going to the washroom," or talking at the back of the room while I was teaching a lesson isn't what I expected students to do. I resolved to introduce a seating plan for the next class.

It was Friday of the first week and I was looking forward to the weekend. I was as exhausted as if I had taught for five days.

Monday, Sept 11

Students usually think that teachers shouldn't make mistakes. New teachers are often embarrassed by mistakes that they do make. It takes maturity to recognize that no one is perfect and that no one knows everything. Sometimes the hardest phrase for a teacher to say is, "I don't know. I'll get back to you about that." They will remember if you don't follow up.

I returned to school with a seating plan in hand. I started each class by rearranging the students, and putting them in alphabetical order. Glen was separated from his cohorts and looked like he'd do some work. It had helped that I'd called home about his continual talking last week.

Most of the students were excellent and they settled into the lessons. Now and then, I made a mistake in calculations as I did the questions on the board. I always have difficulty adding and subtracting before 10:00 am.

The pre-calculus students, especially the boys, were still cocky. One of them, John, was the son of a math professor. He thought he knew more than any math teacher and many of the boys, led by Glen, went to him when they thought that I was not explaining the work correctly. I didn't discourage them, because it's important that students help each other. With thirty-five students in a class, the teacher can't give much individual help.

The basic eleven class was going well but there was a problem with the dress code. The weather was hot and many of the girls liked to wear low-cut tank tops and it was the well-endowed who did so more often. They followed the maxim "If you've got it flaunt it." They also liked to wear low rise pants with cropped tops. When they sat down, the top of their thongs, and sometimes more, showed.

The principal, responding to teachers' complaints, decided it was time for a "beginning of the year" assembly to lay down the school rules. The assembly was scheduled for tomorrow.

Tuesday, Sept 12

Most schools have school-wide rules that must be followed by students. One of the most controversial is the dress code. Some schools have adopted a school uniform while others simply ask for modest dress. The term modest dress changes from year to year and from style to style. During the 1960s girls had to wear skirts or dresses. When the hem line started going up, pant suits were allowed. Jeans for boys and girls were absolutely forbidden. Today modest dress means no abdomens or low-cut tops. Teenagers will always find a type of dress that will challenge the school dress code and force the administration to adapt their rules. Next, I suspect, will be the return of mini skirts, barely covering bottoms.

During today's assembly the current school rules were reinforced.

Item 1: Dress code—No hats, no tank tops, shoulders covered, abdomens covered, etc. We especially don't want to see underwear!
Item 2: Respect—Respect to all, including teachers.
Item 3: Hallways—Don't wander the halls during class time. If you have a free class, leave the building or go to library or cafeteria.

There are the usual platitudes about what a great school Kennedy High is, how the community loves to send their children here, how those who live nearby are always impressed by the behaviour of the students, how the school is the best at sports, and so on. Every student at every school hears the same types of remarks. Fortunately, the children believe it's true and most do their best to live up to this supposed reputation.

Wednesday, Sept 13

When children start a new school it is usually a stressful experience. In grade primary, the most one can hope for is to have the children meet their teacher, find the bathroom and learn where they will sit during the day. Showing them any more of the school is apt to overwhelm them.

In junior high or middle school, the new students are taken on a tour. They are shown the location of the cafeteria, the gym and the administrative offices. They are introduced to the guidance counsellor and other adults who will become important in their lives.

In high school, getting to know the other students and the workings of the student council is the issue. After all, at that age, socialization becomes much more important than the actual day-to-day running of the school. An orientation day for the new grade ten students was scheduled for today.

No classes were to be affected, the teachers were informed, except, it seemed, mine. I had the student council co-presidents in my pre-calculus class. They would be spending the day setting up the games and the barbeque.

Pre-calculus was scheduled for the period before lunch. It wasn't just the co-presidents who would be missing. It appeared that most of the student council was in this class as well. Also, there were a lot of volunteers who were helping with games and cooking the hot dogs. My class was decimated. At least I could now walk around it.

The fun began. My classroom overlooked the parking lot and I could see the children playing games. I wished I was young again.

At the bell, I headed to the staff room, away from the commotion. I'd like to be young, but I am not. I needed to take my lunch break and I needed time to prepare for the afternoon classes.

The rest of the student council was in my grade twelve math class, as were the rest of the volunteers. They had to take the time to clean up. They took all the time they needed to do it well and they did not hurry. When they finished, there was no sign of the games or of lunch. Did they volunteer to help so they would not have to go to class? You bet they did. I would have too, when I was their age. Actually, if I recall correctly, I did and I made sure that I took all the time I needed to make sure the clean up was properly done. It is amazing how an incentive like missing class will get teens to clean.

The only class that wasn't affected was my basic math eleven. Students who struggle in school usually don't volunteer for the fun and games. They don't become an integral part of the social scene of the student body. They often feel alienated because they usually have problems at home and are struggling daily with their lives. They don't have time to have fun. For them, these activities are immature. These students have, sadly, become adults before their time.

Thursday, Sept 14

Of course, every so often a teacher has to test students. No matter how many times students take tests, it often seems that many have never done it before. There is the panic and the last-minute scanning of the work. There is also the regret that they did not have all the notes. There is the borrowing of binders and the expressions of "Do we have to know this?" and "We didn't learn that!" even though an outline was given the day before.

There are several types of tests that a teacher can give. Students are expected to review all their work and be prepared for questions at any time. Of course, they don't and aren't. Therefore, the most disliked is the pop quiz where there is no warning.

A second type and the most liked is the short quiz on a small amount of work. Students only have to know a little bit and the quiz only takes twenty to thirty minutes to complete.

Then there is the major test when a unit of work is complete. Students will study hard for these tests, thinking they are more important than the quizzes. They are not more important, they are just longer because they cover more work. The value of a question on a quiz and the value of a question on a test compared to the overall mark on the course is usually the same.

The final exam is considered the most important of all the testing. Yet the value placed on the exam is typically much less, from twenty to forty percent, of the overall mark. However, students will start preparing for the exam a week or two in advance, the night before for a quiz and maybe a day before for a major test. They can't seem to understand the importance of continual preparation. No matter how many times study skills are discussed in class, cramming is always done.

The pre-calculus and math twelve classes had stopped testing me—at least I thought they had. It was my turn for testing day. I wanted to finish up the units I was teaching so when their permanent teacher returned he could start a new unit. There should always be an easy transition, if possible, for the students.

Testing day is usually an undemanding day for the teacher. All that must be done is to make sure the children don't look at each others' papers. This is not so easy when all a student has to do is glance sideways to see their neighbour's paper. Most students are honest, but there are times when grades are more important than honesty, especially when scholarships are at stake.

I kept a close eye on them. I was still able to work at my desk, however, and there were no problems. Everyone looked at their papers and there were no wandering eyes. These students were cocky and disrespectful at times but they were sincere in their need to do well. I marked the test papers before I went home.

Friday, Sept 15

When an adult has spent five hours a day for two weeks with a group of people even, or perhaps especially, when those people are young, close relationships occur. Probably, though, there is more familiarity on the part of the adult than on the part of the child. Children tend to live in the moment and someone that they cared for a month ago is quickly forgotten. To be fair, this is not always the case and the bonds made between a child and a teacher can continue for a lifetime.

It was Friday and my last day at Kennedy High for this assignment. I would miss the students. I had grown to love them as I always did when I have spent a few days with a particular class.

Leaving was hard, as it always is, but there would be other adventures in the future.

I returned the test papers to the pre-calculus class. There was uproar. Apparently, they believed I marked a question wrong that many thought was right. I went over the question on the board but they insisted I was wrong. Glen, on behalf of his friends, checked with the class authority. John agreed with Glen. John phoned his father, the math professor, who was the class expert on all things mathematical. It was my last day and I had hoped to have a good day. Now my competence was being questioned. The cockiness had not disappeared; it had just been suppressed for a little while.

John returned with the verdict. Dad agreed with me! I was vindicated! The students who questioned my ability apologized. They were so sure they knew more than I but were willing to admit their mistake. I have now become the class authority, but just in time to leave.

The basic eleven class said they would miss me. I tried hard to help them with their math problems. After all, they needed and deserved the best teacher they could get. I wished them luck as I wished all my students at Kennedy High School luck.

I left feeling a little sad. It was Friday and I have already worked for the first two weeks of school but I have no job to go to on Monday.

Monday, Sept 18

Four- and five-year-olds have difficulty with their muscle control. They are slow at every task. Putting on coats and tying shoes is cumbersome. Patience is essential with all age groups, but when working with primaries it is even more vital. Time must be allotted during the day to allow for the extra needs of this age group.

I was asked to teach grade primary French immersion for this week. I informed the vice-principal that I didn't feel comfortable doing French immersion but he said he would rather have someone who could give some structure to the class because it was so early in the year. I remembered some of my university French and this was only grade primary so how hard could it be? After the rudeness of the grade twelves last week, this promised to be refreshing.

Four- and five-year-olds can't seem to eat and play at the same time so their snack had to be eaten first. Snack time started twenty minutes before recess time. It was a long process to get them to take out their recess snack from their backpacks. Some of them stayed for lunch as well and had to be told what part of the packed lunch could be used for a snack. No one could open the granola bars, fruit cups, and so on so I had to go to each student with a pair of scissors and cut them open. It was a wonder that most of them were able to finish in twenty minutes. Of course, while they were eating, they had to have long conversations with each other. Some of the really social children didn't have their snack finished by recess. I let them finish it outside because I really needed that ten-minute break. It was good that the weather was still hot. I didn't have to worry about jackets, snowsuits and boots. The children did have indoor and outdoor shoes, though. I had to make sure they changed their shoes before they went outside. Some of them had laced sneakers. They could tie but were so slow. I helped them with this and out they went.

When they came back in, it was the reverse of the process. They had to change back into the indoor shoes. I had to check this very carefully. Some of the children didn't want to follow this process. They were perfectly happy wearing their outdoor shoes all day. They actually fibbed and said they had changed their shoes when they hadn't. I had to be quite strict with them.

By the time I had told the children to sit and listen, read a story, and talked about the date and weather, the day was over. It was a good thing that I could use the French words that I learned in basic high school French because I don't think I could have done it otherwise. At the end of the day, I was exhausted. I have never seen an overweight grade primary teacher. Now I know why.

Tuesday, Sept 19

Many four- and five-year-olds have great difficulty adjusting to the routines of school. Parents will start preparing them in the summer, telling them what a good time they will have. What some parents forget to tell their children is that school is not just an adventure for a day or two but is a daily occurrence. By the second or third week of school, the adventure is over, school has become routine and some students decide it is time to finish school and return to the practice they have had since birth. In other words, it is time to return to the daycare with which they are familiar, go home with Mom or go to the babysitter. They have spent all their life at these places and that is where they are comfortable.

I was back with the grade primaries again. It didn't take long for them to get used to another teacher. It felt like I had been with them since the beginning of the year. Some of them couldn't remember my name. Often they just called me "Teacher." Sometimes it was "Mrs. Doyle." My favourite, though, was "Mrs. Doll."

The children were just getting used to school but there were a few on any particular day who didn't want to be there. One student, Peter, cried and cried during the morning. His mother brought him back after lunch. When she left, he started running after her. I closed the classroom door and held it shut so he couldn't leave. He screamed for Mom. When he stopped screaming, I let go of the door, and he was gone! Out he ran as fast as his little legs could carry him. Out the back door he went. Fortunately, his mom had not gone far. I stood by the door and yelled, "MOM." She turned around and saw her son running toward her. She waved at me and I hurried back into the classroom, hoping everything was OK there. Who knows what could happen when the teacher is not in the class—fire, pestilence, riot! The other students were fine and not in the least concerned. They were busily telling each other about what they had done at lunch time. At that age, children are so self-absorbed that someone who is troubled does not affect them in the least.

Another child, Donna, was becoming what might be called a bully. She hadn't had much contact with other children and she had difficulty socializing with the other students. Today wasn't a good day for her. She scratched a student and had to be sent to the office for a good talking to. That got her away from the situation but when she returned her behaviour had not changed. She pushed a student and tried to take her crayons. I moved her desk so she was facing the wall and could not look at the others and was given a time out.

Donna cried and cried. She kept saying, "I hate school. I want to be home with my Nana. I don't want to be here." Going to school had become a traumatic experience for her. After she had finished crying and felt better, I let Donna return to the activities with the other children. There were no more problems from Donna for the rest of the time I was there.

Wednesday, Sept 20

Picture day is an important day in the lives of children. The younger children love to dress up and sit proudly while the photographer snaps the picture. As they age, it is not considered fashionable to be seen in anything but ordinary school clothes. By junior high dressing up for picture day is just not done. However, just before they go to sit for their picture, there is a mad rush for the washroom to make sure the hair is just right. They might appear casual but they still must look their best. By the time they are in grade twelve, the students have reverted to the attitude of grade primaries. This is their graduation picture and they must be dressed in their best.

Because it was picture day, all the children were dressed up. Some of the boys wore jackets and ties. All the girls wore dresses and had ribbons in their hair.

There was a set of twins in the class—two girls named Susanne and Natalie. They were identical but their mother either dressed them differently or did their hair differently. For the first couple of days I recognized them by the way they were dressed. Later, I could see little differences in their personalities. Susanne was the more outgoing and confident of the two. She was the leader. Natalie was more sensitive and more of a follower. They seemed surprised that I could call them by name and get it right most of the time. They were obviously not used to that.

When it was time to go to the library to get our pictures taken, I lined up the class and off we went. They walked sedately to the library like the princes and princesses they were. Natalie was "the special student" of the day and led the rest of them. We waited outside the library for previous class to finish. We waited and we waited. Natalie started to get nervous and started to cry. Not good for picture taking.

When we finally got in to the library, Natalie was to have gone first but she was still crying. Her sister took over and told Natalie to wait. Susanne had her picture done. Then the others went one by one. At the end, Natalie still looked miserable. The photographer said that he will wait until retake day to take her picture. It was time for the group picture. Natalie and Susanne sat in the front row. Natalie struggled to give a smile but it was a very unhappy smile.

I sent a note home regarding the picture taking. Because I won't be there for retake day, I won't know the end result. Mom might have to have another picture of Susanne taken in different clothes. The girls are so identical, it would be impossible to tell which twin was which.

Thursday, Sept 21

In all classes, there are differing levels of ability but the differences in primary are often much more noticeable than in the older grades. A child who is not yet five has more difficulty tying shoes than a child who is almost six. Some children have already learned to read before they start school. Some can colour within the lines, others still do not recognize colours. No matter what their abilities, all the children like to colour, listen to stories and trace letters.

Having been in the classroom almost a week, the children were getting used to me. Often I am greeted with hugs and kisses. It was so different from the grade twelves of last week. I received no hugs and kisses there. It didn't take long for this age group to get into a routine. First they listened to a story and then they talked about the day, date and weather. Finally, we did math. They were learning shapes such as squares, circles and so on. Everything, of course, was done in French.

Some of the children were very smart. One little girl, Paula, almost six, could read in English at a grade two level. Another little girl had been speaking French since birth. She was as bilingual as it was possible to be at five years old. She was far more fluent in French than I but was very polite about it. She liked to correct my pronunciation and I thanked her for her help. She grinned and kept helping me for the rest of the week. I always like to improve my French skills and, believe me, her help was welcome.

An eager student, Remy, came in with his mom at lunch time to look for a book. "What are you doing here?" he asked me.

I replied, "I am doing a little work to get ready for this afternoon."

"What about lunch?" he asked.

"I have finished lunch and now I am working."

"I don't want to be a teacher," he pronounced.

In the afternoon, after school, at about 2:30, Remy and his mom come in again while I was correcting papers.

"You're still here? School is over," he said.

"Yes," I said. "I am marking your work."

"I definitely don't want to be a teacher," he replied.

Friday, Sept. 22

When new parents see their baby for the first time they take care to count fingers and toes to make sure they are all there. It is a heartbreak to find that one of your children has a physical disability. The challenges that these new parents have far exceeds the normal challenges that face all new parents. Most parents of the physically challenged are able to meet these tests and, by doing so, exceed the expectations given for their child or in fact for most children.

Unfortunately, once that child starts school, the child with the physical problem can become a target of teasing and prejudice. Anyone who is different is often not understood by the so-called "normal" children.

Shelia was born with a deformity. She was the most beautiful child that I have seen but she had only one hand. Yet, even with this problem, she was one of the most self-reliant students in the class. Her family must have taken extra care to see that she was ready for school. She was more able to hang up her jacket, put on her shoes and open her school bag than the majority of the students.

When I first started with the class, she wasn't a bit self-conscious. Toward the end of the week, I noticed that she was hiding her deformed hand on her lap. She had started to become aware that other children had noticed her differences.

She made a comment to her friend. "I'd like to be a teacher when I grow up."

A boy overheard her. "You can't be a teacher," he said.

"Yes, I can! There are teachers who have only one hand," she responded indignantly.

I didn't say anything but my heart was broken. Prejudice appears to be alive and well in five-year-olds. But I knew that Shelia would be whatever she wanted to be. She wouldn't let the lack of a hand stop her.

I left for the day feeling elated and exhausted. Again, a job was completed and I will miss the hugs and kisses. Children teach me so much more than I teach them. It's part of what keeps me in this profession.

Monday, Sept 25

In junior high or middle school, at the beginning of the year, the eleven- or twelve-year-olds are intimidated by being in a new school. They are the low people on the totem pole and are looked down upon by the seniors in grade nine who have forgotten how they felt only two years before.

The grade eights are always difficult to teach. They are in the middle of their school years and they are no longer intimidated by a new school; however, at the same time, they are not close to graduating. They have little to look forward to. Add to the mix, the developing hormones of thirteen- to fourteen-year-olds and you have a group of students that are easily upset, impatient and unfavourable to change. When a substitute arrives, the children become much more difficult to handle. They recognize that the substitute doesn't know their names and a seating plan doesn't help because they switch their seats to be with friends.

The seniors like to think that they run the school. They are the top students and believe they understand much more than those little freshmen and those immature grade eights. Most of them know better than to cause a commotion in any way. What a difference one year makes.

Today I am teaching at Sherwood Junior High, filling in for core French and health. Sherwood is located in a low to middle socio-economic neighbourhood and a lot of the students have problems at home. Core French is a requirement at junior high but it isn't a subject that holds the interest of many of these children. They don't have to pass it to go on to high school so many spend the class time in R&R.

The first class of the day was grade seven who were an extremely cooperative group. However, it was still first period in the morning, and they probably were not awake yet. The rest of the morning went well but the grade sevens became noisier and livelier as the day progressed proving that I was right—yet again.

Grade eight health was very difficult. As the class started, the paper balls started flying across the room. They were going everywhere. I gave them a good lecture about throwing items at each other, and then I stood in the middle of the room with a garbage can and invited all the students to put their wads of paper in it. The activity changed into an impromptu basketball game and that was the end of the paper throwing. If parents wonder why children use so much paper at this age, then flying paper balls might be the reason.

Grade nine health was totally different. They finished all the assigned work and did puzzles at the end. Teaching grade nines makes teaching junior high worthwhile.

Tuesday, Sept 26

At all ages, bullying is a major problem in today's society. In the primary grades, the bully can often be corrected by talking to parents and getting professional help if need be. Usually, the students are not afraid to stand up to the bully or to walk away. The children are taught to report bullying to the appropriate authorities and most have no fear in doing so. The adults in their lives are their protectors and they are confident that they will be protected. As the children age, they become aware that they cannot always be protected by adults. The problems of bullying then become more pronounced.

By the time they reach junior high, children may not always want to report to adults. They can be fearful for many reasons, including peer pressure and the real fear that their friends and loved ones can be hurt. In addition, the physical development of children at this age is so varied that often the children being bullied can be much smaller than the bullies and they can no longer stand up to them or turn away.

In high school, the children are starting to become adults both physically and mentally. They again begin to realize that the people in authority are in a position to prevent bullying and that the person being bullied has the power to prevent it.

Nottingham Junior High is a school in a middle socio-economic neighbourhood. At this school, I was asked to teach grade eight math and science, which are my favourite subjects. Since I was very comfortable with the curriculum, I was happy to take the job. However, grade eight is grade eight and there are usually problems with that age group, no matter what their background.

Therefore, I was pleasantly surprised when the classes came in. The students were exceptionally cooperative and polite. When I mentioned to the other teachers that this school was proving to be a good school, they disagreed with me. I was told that there were many problems, but the problems show up in the hallways and outside of school, not in the classroom.

I was reminded of the item that was in the news not too long before. A grade eight student from this school had committed suicide. He cited his reason in a letter. He couldn't take the bullying anymore. Apparently, he was being forced to shoplift and was robbed of his money if he brought any to school. Although I didn't see any bullying, I was told it was still going on behind the scenes.

Even so, it was a good day. The students were great and I went home feeling that I had chosen the right profession.

Wednesday, Sept 27

Teenagers develop their own language and every generation has phrases that they hope adults can not understand. "Groovy" from the 1960s is one of the common examples. Because teenagers have much faster communication in the computer age, the teenage language develops far more quickly than in the past. A phrase that was new last month would now be obsolete. Hence the phrase "That was sooo last year."

Ridge Road Junior High is in a different part of the city than the previous schools. The students here are similar to those at Sherwood but also include a few students from upper-middle socio-economic families. This makes for a difficult mix with the more affluent conflicting with the poorer students. There isn't a lot of tolerance for differences among the classes at this age group and arguments and fights will often break out.

As usual, the first class was a great class because the children have not yet woken up. During the rest of the day very little work was done, but they didn't really misbehave in any other way. As they were leaving, Joey said, "See you, funky grandma." What did that mean? I hadn't heard that phrase before. Was that a compliment like "You're all that and a bag of chips"? But that phrase is sooo last year. Ya know what I'm talkin' bout.

Thursday, Sept 28

What a difference a year or two makes. By the time children are ready to enter high school they have matured to a point where their changing hormones no longer control their lives. For the most part, they can control the hormones. That is not to say that the search for a boy- or girlfriend is not important. Indeed, the biological need to find a mate can often be overwhelming. However, at this age, most children will be able to recognize that they must first complete their education. Most recognize that, in a few short years, this part of their lives will be finished.

For some children, leaving the security of school that has so dominated all their lives can be scary and they may find ways to extend their high school years; however, these children are in the minority. Therefore, high school is so much easier to teach than junior high. There are fewer discipline problems in the classroom. Very seldom do you see flying objects and the students are usually much more respectful.

I was going to be teaching business at the high school level, grade ten being the first class. I made sure I was seen in the hall and many of the students didn't come to class. I always do that in high school because I don't want to have them in class if they don't want to be there. It makes for a much better lesson because the troublemakers have decided to spend their time in the cafeteria.

For most of the day, the students were well behaved and

worked hard. There is very little for me to do and I found the day long and tedious. At one point, I was called on to fix a printer and it was pleasant to have something to do. The rest of the time, I just watched them work. I always make sure that I have a few crossword puzzles to do on these days. Sometimes I can read a book if the classes are really good. Occasionally, I will write a poem or two.

Friday, Sept 29

In any school, allowing food in the classroom is a controversial issue. Children get hungry, and not just at the specified times of recess and lunch. What is the correct policy to follow? Do we allow water? Of course, we can't deny children a drink of water and it is better that they have water in the class than take time away from instruction to get a drink. Do we allow juice? Usually not, because if it is spilled it becomes sticky and hard to clean.

What about food? Is it healthy to allow children to get really hungry and then eat excessively at break time? Studies have shown that hungry children have difficulty concentrating and achieving success at school. Should we allow them to snack on carrot sticks and apple slices when necessary? At present, most schools do not allow food in the classrooms. Not only do children have difficulty concentrating but they will also try to sneak snacks and these snacks are usually unhealthy. Are the rules about eating in the classroom producing bad habits that eventually lead to obesity?

Already it is Friday and I am back at Ridge Road Junior High. It had turned into a zoo because there were a lot of animal noises (moos, quacks, oinks, etc.) coming from the back of the room. I told the grade nine boys that I'd be happy to let them practice their animal sounds after school. Suddenly the zoo disappeared and the room became a place of learning again.

Mike, a student, must have been hungry. His choice of snack was sunflower seeds which is not unhealthy in itself. Unfortunately, he didn't eat the husks and having no garbage can nearby, he spit them on the floor. When asked, he refused to pick up the shells so I sent him to the office for defiance. He returned a few minutes later carrying a broom. Mike helpfully cleaned up the sunflower seeds and then swept the rest of the classroom floor before he settled into his lessons which he completed with renewed gusto.

OCTOBER

Monday, Oct 2

Between the ages of twelve and fifteen, children often find that their changing hormones overpower common sense. They are still learning what constitutes appropriate behaviour, especially that which will win the opposite sex. Unsuitable behaviour is frequent. Sometimes I think that at junior high the classes should be separated by sex—all boys in one class and all girls in another. Perhaps this would overcome a lot of the behaviour problems but, at the same time, I know it would create new ones.

I am back at Nottingham teaching grade seven. This class still seems intimidated by being in a new school. They are still very young and most have just started the process of puberty. They were noisy though and I had to raise my voice to make myself heard, but when they realized I was there, they did quiet down. Many students in this class are still in the "tattle-tale" stage and use this as a way to get attention from their heartthrob of the month.

Mary said, "He is making faces at me!"

Gorge replied, "Mary won't give me my pencil sharpener."

After I solved the pencil-sharpener issue, the class asked many questions and requested help on their exercises. How refreshing it was to be able to do my job. What a difference from the animal zoo of yesterday!

Tuesday, Oct 3

Sex, to twelve- and thirteen-year-olds, is an uncomfortable subject. The boys, especially, like to talk about it but, because of their embarrassment, they bring up the subject in a comedic setting. Sometimes they don't understand the true meaning of the words they use but, the more laughs they get; the greater their esteem rises in their own minds.

Today, we read about the environment and eco-systems in grade seven science.

Invariably, when I am substituting in a class that is doing this section, one bright boy will replace the word "organism" with "orgasm." I am always prepared to quickly correct the "error" before there is too much laughter and the class gets out of control.

This time, however, I was too quick to correct. The reader, Barry, read properly and well. He said, "Organism."

"Orgasm," I corrected much to the delight of the class and to my embarrassment.

Wednesday, Oct 4

Problems with a school building create turmoil within a community. If a school has to be closed due to fire, mould or other problems, then classes have to be shuffled. Sometimes an empty building can be found but usually the classes share with another school. This leads to split shifts.

At 10:00 a.m. this morning I received a call to teach at Sunnybrae High. Sunnybrae was undergoing renovations so it was sharing with Parkview High. Sunnybrae was taking the 1:00–6:30 afternoon shift.

I arrived at 12:30 to complete chaos. When fifteen hundred

teenagers finish school at 12:10 and another fifteen hundred arrive for 1:00 then there is a bit of a problem. There were school busses lined up everywhere. To me, it seemed that those leaving could not get out and those coming in were blocking the driveway. In addition, one hundred teachers and support staff were changing shifts. Their cars added to the confusion. Furthermore there were a few older students who had their own or, more likely, their parents' cars. How it was done, I don't know, but by 1:00 there was a complete shift change and everything was ready to go.

As is always the case, the less time you have to do work, the more time it will take you. After having supervision duty for the first half of first period, I had to make photocopies for the next class. First I had to make a transparency to show with an overhead projector. I could not find one so I had to inquire at the office. Then I couldn't get the photocopier to work because I didn't have the needed password. I was given a password by the vice principal and started to photocopy. After about thirty copies, I realized that I had put the paper in backwards and had to start again. The photocopier ran out of staples so I had to staple seventy tests by hand. The standard stapler in the workroom had no staples. I used the heavy duty one which ran out after twenty copies. I went back to the office for the third time, found the staples and finished the job just as the bell rang for the next class.

The first class I taught was basic math. They were totally disinterested and didn't want to copy the notes the teacher left. One student had "anger management" problems and kept yelling at me about the work I was asking the class to do. I told him that that issue was between him and his regular teacher who had left the work. Although he settled down, he was still angry when he left the class.

The next two classes were wonderful. The students addressed

me by "Miss." When I helped them, they replied, "Thank you, Miss." It was so pleasant to hear but not as much fun as "funky grandma."

Thursday, Oct 5

In my community, there are two classes of schools. The schools that were built or renovated in the last ten to fifteen years are technologically advanced. They are wired for the computer age. They have a projector in each class which can be used to broadcast video announcements. In addition, each classroom contains at least one computer which can be used to show web pages and presentations through the projector. Of course there are VCR and DVD capabilities in every room as well. The students have the opportunity to use computers on a daily basis and are comfortable with them.

Schools that are older do not have these advantages. To be fair, there are computer labs which can be booked by the classroom teacher but teachers and students do not have the same ease of access to technology.

Meadowbrook Junior High is a new school and was built with all the bells and whistles. The grade eight class, to whom I was teaching math and science, were a great group.

One young man, Evatt, finished his work early and kept turning around. There was a girl a few seats over and he was trying to get her attention. I had to tell him a few times to turn back. Evatt said, "I keep looking the other way because you have such a beautiful face."

I was ready to reply, "Flattery will get you nowhere," but I started to laugh. I changed it to "Flattery will help a little bit." Some ladies' men start at a very early age.

In the afternoon we watched a movie called *Osmosis Jones*, a cartoon with a strong message about leading a good lifestyle. The students were so enthralled with the movie that they forgot where they were. When it was over they got up and left as they would do if they were in a theatre. I had to chase them back into the classroom.

Friday, Oct. 6

For a teenager, being prepared for a day at high school often doesn't mean having homework done and books packed. Although this is part of the preparation, it's certainly not the whole. Both boys and girls will spend much of their time picking out the best outfit to wear and making sure all is clean and ready to go. In the morning, hair styling for both sexes and makeup for girls, and a few boys, take much of their time. The older teens would rather be late for school than be seen in the not-so-perfect outfit and having a bad hair day.

Today I was back at Sunnybrae High with good classes and no discipline problems. At the beginning of one class, I noticed Lisa, a female student, had blue eye shadow drawn in large circles around her eyes and looking much like a racoon. I was concerned, thinking she might be covering a bruise, a sign of child abuse.

I said to Lisa, "What's with the eyes?"

She replied, "It's THE LOOK, you know!"

I examined THE LOOK carefully and unobtrusively. I could see no sign of bruises.

Tuesday, Oct 10

As much as we want to prevent it, and try to avoid it, children will always label others. Although the negative labels of the past such as retard and SPED (special education) are no longer used, children will frequently invent new ones to label those that they see as different. In order to increase their self-esteem, these labels will be adopted by the less academically inclined and be used as an excuse for not doing well.

After a nice long weekend celebrating the Thanksgiving Holiday, I returned to Sunnybrae High this afternoon. You know, it's great to be paid for a full day and not have to start until 1:00. Although I got home early in the evening, it is a treat to be able to sleep in.

For the first two periods, I was asked to put notes on the board for the students to copy. For each class, I wrote for over an hour until my arm throbbed. Some of the students started to complain about the amount of notes they had to copy. I told them to stop complaining. After all, I had to do it twice!

The third class was a basic math class. They didn't want to take notes because, as they told me, they knew it all. They didn't want me to explain the exercises because, as they told me, they knew how to do it. I gave them a hand-in assignment but they didn't do it because, as they told me, they had done it already. Their own nickname for their class was the "Flunkies," because, as they told me, many of them had taken the course several times.

Wednesday, Oct 11

To many children, especially those who have struggling home lives, school is a place of refuge. It is the only place they know where they can relax, discuss issues with friends who have similar problems, and unwind. Unfortunately, this leads to a decrease in academic standards for those children.

Today, I went to Ridge Road where I taught grade seven. This particular group of children fit the above description. They had no real discipline problems but they liked to discuss their home problems with each other. As a result, the conversation became far more important than the assigned work. It is not that they didn't want to do any work, but their problems, on this day, were taking precedence. Any assignments given were replaced by talking, talking and more talking. When I spoke to them, they listened and were polite but they were just a very sociable group with many, many issues.

Thursday, Oct 12

Although education is a serious business, there are times when students must let their hair down. In high school, this is done much more appropriately than in junior high. They are much more adept at teasing the teacher and creating a relaxed atmosphere than they are in the younger grades. Classmates can appreciate a good joke, or a bad one, without getting carried away and causing a major disturbance.

My assignment for today is Parkview High which is doing the early shift. Since I am not a morning person, having to be at school for 7:00 in the morning was difficult. On the plus side, however, I was done at 12:30 and had the afternoon to enjoy.

I was filling in for a teacher who had fifty percent math and fifty percent resource. I found, with relief, that the first period was preparation. Since, thankfully, all the material was ready for me, I spent the time reviewing the lessons and waking up.

The next two classes were in resource. In resource, because of the extra help provided, there are far fewer students. For period number two, I reviewed for a test with one student. Third period, I helped two students finish a different test. I had seen a total of three students in three periods. I started to wonder if it could it get any better and still be paid.

For the rest of the day, I taught math. There were thirty students in the class, and thirty voices going at once. What a racket! I added mine to the noise and had to yell to be heard. After I spoke to them about the noise, they would quiet down for a few minutes and start all over again. They were good sports, though, and, as all teenagers, liked to have fun. As I walked by one table, I was told I had a "henway" in my hair. Four eager young faces were looking at me with their eyes sparkling.

Even though I had heard the joke many times, I knew I had to respond so I said, "What's a henway?"

"About the same as a chicken."

Friday, Oct 13

When a boy and a girl in junior high start to have feelings for each other, it often comes with inappropriate behaviour. They are not yet ready to commit to a one-on-one relationship. They can't or won't ask each other for a date. Firstly, they don't know how, and secondly, they probably are not allowed. The best they can do, usually, is arrange to meet each other at the mall or at a school event. Often, it doesn't even go that far. But during recess, between classes and lunch time, the relationship will continue to evolve.

At a junior high today, I noticed a boy running in the hall. Behind him there was a girl who was chasing him and trying to hit him with her shoe. What did he do that made her so angry? Indeed, was she really angry or just trying to get attention? It was probably the latter. I separated the two. Ah, young love.

After that incident, I earned the reputation of being "cool" and another boy, Phil, took the time to teach me the "cool" handshake. I had been initiated into "the club" at that school.

Monday, Oct 16

My school board requires a credit in fine arts as a graduation requirement. Students have the choice of taking art, drama, music or dance. For many students, this is an opportunity of which to take full advantage. For others fine arts is a subject to be avoided at any cost. If one doesn't have any natural talents in this area, fine arts can be a struggle. As a consequence, grade ten classes are the most difficult, while the grade eleven and twelve classes are populated with many talented children.

Dover High is a relatively new school in a middle to upper socio-economic neighbourhood. Since it's a new school it's also technically advanced and has the reputation of being called the "elitist school." It usually is a pleasure to teach at Dover High.

Today I am replacing the art teacher but, even though the school has a great reputation, the grade ten art class didn't live up to it. They were working with plasticene and making some beautiful and scenic plaques. However, plasticene can easily be formed into small balls and thrown across the room. Many grade ten students were talented with that skill.

In grade eleven and twelve, the students worked hard for most of the class. Much of the time, they didn't appear to know I was there. My only function, after introducing the lesson, was to give them supplies from the supply cupboard.

Tuesday, Oct 17

When a substitute enters a class, junior high students will take advantage of the situation. One of the easiest ways is to juggle the class seating plan. Although a seating plan may be left, it is difficult for a substitute to know if the correct student is in the correct seat. Calling a student by the wrong name can be a cause of much amusement.

At Parkview Junior High I had grade nine, math, science and French. Some of the grade nines at this school were quite talkative. In this class, they also didn't want to follow the set seating plan, but wanted this chance to sit with their friends.

At the beginning of the class, there were two boys fighting over a seat. Franklyn was trying to remove Julian's binder from his desk but Julian had fast hold of his binder. I walked over, tapped Franklyn on the shoulder, and said, "May I cut in?"To my astonishment and pleasure, Franklyn let the binder go and Julian moved to another seat. There were no protestations or arguments but Franklyn was not finished with his attention-getting behaviour.

Franklyn decided he would try a new look. He tucked the bottom of his shirt into his neckline, exposing his abdomen. He pulled his jeans down on his hips, showing off his fancy under shorts. When I told him it was more exposure than I cared to see, he returned to a more modest dress, having gained some attention but Franklyn was not yet satisfied.

A few minutes later, Franklyn jumped up and out of his seat. I touched his shoulder and he immediately sat down, protesting about sexual harassment. As he sat, he lost his balance and ended with his hands on the floor. I was wearing a full skirt, about mid-calf length. He inadvertently happened to glance up. I knew that my skirt was below his range of vision, but, taking advantage of the opportunity, I teasingly said, "Now that's sexual harassment!"

Franklyn turned bright red. He protested, "I didn't see anything!" He covered his face with his hands, and stayed that way for a full ten minutes. There were no more problems from Franklyn.

Wednesday, Oct 18

Because of their immaturity, many junior high students do not always remember that all actions have consequences. Sometimes what has started as a simple prank can lead to far-reaching problems, not only for those who are the recipients of the prank but also for themselves. Children will often say that they didn't mean for anyone to get hurt, and indeed this is true. Unfortunately, it is usually the child who gets hurt the most for not being able to understand where his or her actions will lead.

I returned to Ridge Road Junior High, but this time to teach technology education. Unfortunately, Ridge Road is one of the technologically disadvantaged schools with computers that were at least five years old and awfully slow. The students were learning drafting with a CAD program.

Bert, a grade eight student, had to be sent to the office for unruly behaviour. Within ten minutes he was back. He went to a computer and worked quietly enabling me to help the other students. When I walked by Bert's computer, I noticed the reason for his quiet behaviour. He was on a chat line. I immediately asked him to get off and go back to CAD and he promptly complied. A few minutes later, he was back chatting. I tried to phone the office about this defiance but there was no answer.

Suddenly, there was an announcement asking teachers to make note of anyone who was on the internet. I immediately suspected Bert. Apparently he was sending obscene messages to other teachers and the vice-principal. Poor Bert, he earned two day's suspension.

Thursday, Oct. 19

Supervising students, otherwise known as duty, can be invigorating, boring, and rewarding. In elementary, the goal of many is to hold the teacher's hand. Since a teacher has only two hands, some of them will grab a corner of a coat. Others will hold the hand of a student who is holding the teacher's hand. It's as if the power of the teacher flows through each student to the next like electricity flows through wire.

In junior high, it is not cool to be seen with a teacher on duty but students will strike up a conversation if they are so excited they have forgotten to be cool. Others will stay in the class at recess or lunch so they can make conversation without being seen by their peers.

In high school, duty often consists of keeping an eye on one section of the cafeteria or the hallway. The teacher usually stands alone in the cafeteria but can be found in intense conversation with a student in the hallway.

I returned to Dover High where I would be teaching grade eleven advanced math and pre-calculus. Needless to say, I had wonderful classes. To top it off, I had the second half of cafeteria duty. By the time I entered the cafeteria, there were only six students eating. The rest had finished and had either gone outside or to the library. I spent the time cleaning up the residue of the lunches that the students had left. Next to one half-eaten lunch I found three nickels. I went home with a $0.15 tip!

Friday, Oct 20

Students who take advanced courses such as French immersion are often the truly academically gifted. Sometimes parents, who in the mistaken belief that they have produced one of these types of children, will convince their child to enrol in the French immersion courses. Unfortunately, these children are not able to cope with the amount of work required and have to leave the following year. However, if a child is doing well, by the time that child is in the second or third year of French immersion he or she will be well on the way to being bilingual.

For a change, I started the day without work. Then I received a call at 10:52 to be at Parkview Junior High for 11:00. Needless to say, I was late.

For once there were no red lights and I arrived at 11:35 where I discovered that I would be teaching grade nine French immersion. I was able to do grade primary French immersion but grade nine is a little different. These students had been in French immersion since at least grade seven but even they occasionally enjoyed a little break from speaking French. They were very cooperative and very willing to help me practice the little French I do know. They didn't laugh at my accent and respected my willingness to learn from them.

The afternoon class tried to misbehave. They knew that a substitute teacher will give them the opportunity for more fun than usual, simply because the substitute does not know all their names or the school procedures. They threw bits of eraser around the class but they were unskilled. I caught the culprits and after a warning they stopped. For the rest of the afternoon, the students whispered while they worked and giggled quietly. It was the best misbehaviour most of them could manage.

Monday, Oct. 23

In today's society teenagers listen to music and watch many videos that use inappropriate language. In the more conservative society of the mid-twentieth century, any programs with that type of language would immediately be banned. The use of the word "fuck" would almost never be heard and its use would be cause for alarm and perhaps arrest. Even the use of profanity in public was illegal!

In the mores of today, much has changed. When teenagers are speaking to each other, they use language that would have shocked their grandparents in earlier times. The adolescent realizes that the use of this language will cause problems if used in the classroom and on formal occasions, but when chatting with themselves, it is a such commonplace occurrence that is used unconsciously.

Today, I was back at Dover High teaching the advanced eleven and pre-calculus classes again. The students started asking questions and were pleased that I was able to help them with their math. While I was walking in the hall between classes, I came upon a group of teenagers who were talking with each other. One jokingly said, "You fucking bastard."

I tapped him on his shoulder as I walked past. I said, "Be careful what you say." The group laughed and the guilty party became extremely flustered. He had no idea there was a teacher who was so close.

Tuesday, Oct 24

Most elementary students love to go to music class. They are not self-conscious in their talents. Singing and learning rhythm is part of their life and they usually participate with gusto. But, if there is one thing that I absolutely cannot do, it's sing. I cannot carry a note. I actually took singing lessons for a year as a child and my parents were advised to stop wasting their money! In grade four, I was, in fact, asked not to sing at the school concert because I was so off key, I was ruining the presentation. However, I can play the piano a little bit and with practice can teach a class if I ask the best singers to lead. Nevertheless, this only works for a short time and on simple tunes.

Today I was asked to teach primary to grade six music. Because it's so close to Halloween we sang songs like "Boogie, Woogie Ghost," "Skin and Bones" and "Witches Broom."

The grade primaries were a little talkative. When it was time to go back to class, I told them that they should pretend they were grade fours and walk with their hands by their sides and very quietly. "Better yet," said one little girl, Emily, "We should walk like junior highs!"

The grade six class was learning to read notes. One little boy, Evan, complained that he could not understand the notes. "I'm learning the electric guitar," he said. "The notes are different!"

Wednesday, Oct 25

Children don't understand the responsibilities of adults. They often feel that the work adults do is always fun. After all, they have chosen the job they are doing every day and surely they must really enjoy every minute of it. Adults almost never burden their children with the problems of the work place and so this adds to the illusion. Learning new information in school is work. Earning money is fun.

This day proved to be one of the more difficult ones. I was teaching core French and everything went well in the morning but by lunch time there was chaos.

A student released a stink bomb in the upstairs hallway. I kept the classroom door closed and hoped for the best. Another stink bomb was released near the gym. The administration was having a difficult time rounding up the culprits and at lunch time asked us to keep our eyes open. During homeroom period in the afternoon a student or students released another one at the back of my classroom. Fortunately, I had a preparation period next class. I opened all the windows, set up a fan, went to the office to report it and then waited in the staff room. When I returned for the next class, the smell was gone. However, I and some other students were suffering allergic reactions to the smell and things didn't go well. Two girls were too sick to stay in class. Several people suffered burning eyes and many, including me, had headaches.

Terry, a conscientious boy, said, "I can't work; I have a headache."

"So do I," I replied, "but I am working."

"No, you're not," was the response.

"I'm not?" I queried, thinking that this was my hardest day so far this year.

"No you're not," he answered. "You're just talking!"

Thursday, Oct 26

The graduating class always has much work to do. Although marks are important and first-term marks are used for university entrance and scholarships, one of the main concerns at this time of year is the yearbook. It must be sent to the publisher fairly quickly if it is to be ready by graduation so information needed for each senior student must be collected in the fall.

After the problems of yesterday, it was a relief to be going to high school. In addition, it was Sunnybrae High so I could sleep late which helped to get rid of the headache.

I taught grade twelve English and twelve computer studies. The teacher had laid out all the work and all I had to do was supervise. Everyone worked well and I had very little to do. Days like this are boring, but today, I needed the rest. I had time to do crossword puzzles and read a little bit.

During the last class, the pre-calculus students were asked to provide autobiographical information for the yearbook. They were a little noisy but were having fun. Suddenly I heard a scream. I thought the students were getting a little carried away and I must have had a stern look on my face. The class laughed at my expression. Apparently they were used to that noise. It was a girl sneezing!

Tomorrow is Conference Day. This happens once a year and is for all teachers in the province. For me it's a holiday. I could go to conference if I wanted to but I'd rather have the time off, especially considering the fact that I'd not be paid and, in addition, I'd have to pay for the conference out of my own pocket.

Monday, Oct 30

Every generation must rebel against the adults of the previous generation. One of the most popular and least disruptive rebellions is dress style. In years past, all the teenagers would adopt a certain style. After much ado, the style would then be modified to fit the adults and teenagers would have to adopt another style. Today the teens are more individualistic and will adopt one of several different styles. Or, indeed, wear one style on one day and another on the next.

Today I had a grade five elementary class who were a good group of children. They were, however, trying to imitate teens in their style of dress.

One boy, Rien, asked to go to the washroom. I gave him permission. I noticed that he had his sweat pants down on his hips, copying some older hero. When he got to the door, he had difficulty opening it. In the struggle, his pants fell down around his ankles. I couldn't help it. I laughed out loud. Rein quickly pulled up his pants and slipped out of the classroom.

When he came back after lunch he now wore a pair of jeans tightly belted at his waist.

Tuesday, Oct 31

All children from grade primary to grade twelve want to celebrate Halloween but the method of celebration depends on the class and the age group. A Halloween party with fifteen excited primaries can be just as, if not more, difficult than watching a spooky movie with junior high students or holding a costume contest with high school students.

Today, though, I am at Parkview High which is the school that starts at 7:30 and goes to 12:00. Therefore, I thought, the excitement about Halloween would probably not affect the classes.

I was asked to teach drama and career & life management. I know a little about drama. In university, I was in one play where I had a line as a maid, "Dinner is served." I really don't think, though, that this is enough for me to teach drama on a long-term basis.

There was no problem today. The classes watched the movie,

Dead Poet's Society and were to examine the characterization in the movie. Since I had not seen this movie before, it was great to be able to watch it with them.

Despite their age and the early morning start, some students were dressed for Halloween. I recognized a tiger and a pumpkin but I was not sure about some of the others. Some of the girls were wearing pyjama bottoms. I knew this is a comfortable style that girls, and some boys, seemed to be wearing more and more often. So, are the pyjama bottoms an everyday occurrence or were they a costume? I think the one wearing "Winnie the Pooh" slippers was dressed up but how can one be sure?

Two young men wanted to borrow black blazers from the costume room. They said they were wearing them for Halloween. Were they dressed as businessmen or perhaps imitating life insurance salesmen or lawyers. Now, that would be scary!

Some of the girls had dyed black hair and black lipstick and were wearing black clothes. Was that a Halloween costume or were they wearing yet another outfit that some students like to adopt in high school? Some days it's hard to tell!

NOVEMBER

Wednesday, Nov 1

By the time they reach high school, a few students have refined their humour to the point that they could be stand up comedians. They have had practice at variety shows, in class, and with their friends. Sometimes, they still need the attention in class and will use their talent to draw it. The drama class is an excellent outlet for their talents.

At Parkview High, I had the opportunity to watch the rest of "Dead Poet's Society"—twice. In one class, the students were quite talkative and it was difficult to keep them quiet. In another, you could hear a pin drop. It was like night and day.

Colin was in the first class. He simply couldn't stop talking. When I asked him to be quiet for the umpteenth time, I reminded him that he had questions on characterization that had to be done after the movie.

He answered, "When you have to do a report on a movie, simply read the book."

Thursday, Nov 2

Core French in elementary grades is an exciting class for children. It gives them the opportunity to learn a new language and, at the same time, play games. Core French is taught the way a first language is learned. To start, all is oral and a baby has fun while learning and listening. Later, the toddler starts speaking but the words are difficult to understand. Sentences will come later. Reading and writing of the language comes later still. Thus, in elementary, the emphasis is on playing games, having fun and speaking.

The core French classes, grades four to six that I was teaching today were delightful. They were so enthusiastic about learning that I was able to conduct the entire class in French since I only had to use simple words.

Nellie, from grade four asked, "Teacher, what is your real name."

"Mrs. Doyle," I replied.

"No," said Nellie, "Your real real name."

"Mrs. Doyle is my real name," I said.

"No, your other real name."

"Oh," I said, finally understanding. "You mean my first name!"

Friday, Nov 3

When students in elementary school have been together for six or seven years, they make strong bonds with each other. Probably ninety-five percent of each class has known each other most of their lives. When they go on to junior high or middle school, they mix with one or two other groups that have also made strong bonds. Suddenly, they are in a class where they may know only one-third of the students. Their pride in being a part of a small community changes to the fear and apprehension of the unknown—the unknown of new procedures, new teachers and new classmates. It is difficult for them to create the same bonds that they shared in the elementary grades.

I am doing elementary core French again at a different school called Mill Cove Consolidated. This school is a primary to nine school. The students in grades primary to six are wonderful. When they start grade seven, students from another neighbourhood join them and conflicts result. This makes the junior high section of the school very difficult.

Not only was I teaching French, I also did two classes of resource. The resource students read books to me and I asked them about the stories. The two students in grade three wanted to embellish the stories. For example, in one story, a child was given a rope ladder so she could climb to a tree house. The student said she was given a ladder and other toys. In another story, there was a picture of a bear with glasses. This was father bear. The student insisted it was grandfather bear because the glasses made him a grandfather.

In grade four French, Martin was making animal noises. I asked him to be quiet. Martin replied, "But I want to be a cow."

I told him, "You can be a cow, but you must chew your cud quietly." The mooing stopped.

Monday, Nov 6

Travelling from one school to another on a daily basis can be a cause of confusion for the substitute teacher. Every school has a different schedule and different rules. Schools can start at any time from 7:30 to 9:30. Lunch time can be held anywhere from 11:00 to 1:00 and dismissal can be from 2:00 to 4:00. This, of course, doesn't include the two schools that are sharing one building and are on split shift.

At Dover High, I am teaching pre-calculus and eleven advanced math. It felt empowering to actually have a math lesson to teach and I had a lot of fun.

Unfortunately, though, I got confused with the times. I thought it was lunch period and I was one-half hour late for a class. Thankfully, the students and staff were understanding and there were no problems. It was a good way to finish up a week. TGIF

Tuesday, Nov 7

Once in a while, one needs an extra day off to enjoy the simple pleasures of life. Snow days are an excuse to do just that. Students think they are the only ones who enjoy sleeping in on snow days and teachers must really regret the time they have to take away from work. I hate to disillusion them, but one of the big contests in many staff rooms is the snow day lottery.

Today, we woke up to a snowstorm. All schools were cancelled. There is no work today. It was great to be home but there goes a day's pay. Substitutes don't get paid if there is no work. This was to be a good day because I was going to Dover High again but an even better day is staying home, sitting in front of the fireplace, drinking cocoa and reading a good book.

Wednesday, Nov 8

Safety in the schools is a large issue. It is important that children feel as safe in the classroom as they do in their homes. To keep them safe, no unknown visitor is allowed on the school premises. Most schools have various lockdown procedures, from locking all outside doors to locking the classroom door and not allowing anyone in the hallway. Which procedure is used depends on the situation in question.

At Parkview Junior High, I had to deal with an incident that left me feeling quite nervous. I was given recess supervision so, at the bell, I went outside. There was a taxi parked by the front door. The driver, in his late forties, got out of the taxi and lit a cigarette. He stood by his car for a few minutes smoking the cigarette, drinking coffee and watching the children. I thought, perhaps, he was waiting for a fare but no one appeared. I didn't want to leave the children so I stood near him, hoping that someone would come. Finally, another teacher appeared so I immediately went inside and reported him to the office. The principal spoke to him and he drove away. It was creepy!

Thursday, Nov 9

In almost every class, there are one or two students who would try the patience of the most patient individual. In some classes there are several more. Although the teacher does his or her best to keep things under control, at times these students will cause disruptions that prevent any learning taking place. It affects each person, not only the teacher but also the rest of the students in the class, in different ways.

I was asked to teach the worst class at Mill Cove Consolidated. Five or six of the students (about twenty percent) in this class had no self-discipline. They were up and down in their seats. They were always right and refused to take direction from authority. Work is something they didn't believe in. In short, they had no respect for anyone in the class.

Because many students are followers, another thirty percent of the class (ten students) were following their lead. They copied the antics of the misbehaving students, becoming problems themselves. Although they didn't want to show disrespect, they felt that they could get away with not doing the assigned work and spend the day having a good time.

Another twenty-five percent of the students were excellent. In spite of the noise and the antics of the majority, they were able to concentrate and do their work. Some of them asked to work in the hallway where it was quieter. Others ignored the chaos and did their work at their desks. They were the other group of leaders in the class who had goals and would not let anyone or anything prevent them from reaching them.

The other twenty-five percent of the class had given up. They didn't join in with the behaviour issues and so showed their respect for the others in the class and for authority but, at the same time, they did no work. One said that he didn't believe in copying notes. Another said that, because of the noise, which apparently occurred on a daily basis, it was too difficult to learn in that class.

Friday, Nov 10

Remembrance Day is an important event in the school year. Today's generation often do not hear stories of war first hand. Many of their parents and even grandparents, luckily, have never experienced war. Some hear war stories from their great grandparents and they retain great respect for the sacrifices they made. To keep the younger generations informed of these sacrifices, teachers and veterans work together to maintain the importance of Remembrance Day.

Quaker Grove, a pre-primary to nine school, is in an area where approximately seventy-five percent of the families are on social assistance while the other twenty-five percent have low income jobs. The students at this school have a lot of problems at home and, of course, bring those problems to school. The teachers do their best to improve the situation for all the children, but because of their home life, these children tend to fall behind academically.

This afternoon, the local legion presented a Remembrance Day ceremony to the entire school. I have attended many of these ceremonies. Always, there is the same type of scenario. Most of the students are highly respectful and listen with interest and participate in the program. Some of the students listen with the coercion and supervision of the teachers. A few demonstrate no interest in the sacrifices made by the veterans and have to be asked to leave the ceremony.

At Quaker Grove the ceremony was outstanding. Every child, from the age of 4 to 15 sat on the floor of the gymnasium. When the ceremony started they stood respectfully and sang "O Canada." During the minute of silence, there was not one giggle, not one cough, not even the shuffle of little feet. I have never seen such a wonderful group of children. Congratulations, Quaker Grove.

Tuesday, Nov 14

Although war is necessary to preserve our freedoms when they are threatened, there are always losses on both sides. Children often don't know the reasons for war, but they always assume that there is a winner and a loser. Of course, in any war games they play, they will be on the winning side.

Quell surprise! When I arrived at Mill Cove, I was switched from the grade eight I had the previous week to grade nine French immersion with some core French thrown in. Apparently, the administration wanted to show me that not all the classes in the school were bad. I knew that but I was pleased to be taken from the worst class in the school and be put in the best.

One grade nine core French class had, however, started a war. They were throwing pencils at each other and the losers were the ones who got caught by the substitute. I caught four, two from each side. They all had to write apology letters.

Wednesday, Nov 15

Artists and their art come in many shapes and sizes. Some of the art is quite imaginative and some would question what art actually is. Is art the expression of one's emotions or is art that painting over the mantelpiece that improves the look of your living room? Both are art but the former allows the freedom of thought while the latter allows the freedom of having enough money for eating. Sometimes the two go together but often the expression of feeling does not produce a picture that most would buy and display. The study of art in high school allows students to explore their feelings and gives them the opportunity to produce pieces that reflect their present condition.

I arrived at Parkview High for 7:00 but the vice-principal had forgotten who I was filling in for. That was fine with me. I could wait, especially at that hour in the morning. I just hoped I could teach the subject without any time for preparation.

Apparently, I was to be the art teacher. The first class, grade eleven, was a little restless because I was fifteen minutes late but they settled down quickly. However, a group of girls started to laugh while they were drawing in their sketchbooks. Charlotte was laughing so hard she started to cry and her mascara started to run. She wiped her eyes with her sweater causing the mascara to spread over her face. This resulted in even more laughter from her friends.

I walked over to the group. Charlotte had mascara all around her eyes, on her cheeks and even on her chin. "Charlotte," I suggested, "perhaps you should go to the washroom to wash your face."

"That's OK," said Charlotte, "I'll wipe my face in my sketch book and create mascara art."

I supposed this was a good art idea but it made her face look even worse. Finally a friend agreed to go with her to clean her face. By this time, Charlotte was laughing so hard, she could hardly walk and needed assistance. When Charlotte and her friend came back to class, all was calm and they continued to work. Charlotte finished her mascara art before she left the class.

Thursday, Nov 16

Hockey is considered Canada's unofficial national sport. During the winter, hockey is often the conversation before and during school in junior and senior high. If the talk is not about the games they played the night before or the practice or road hockey game they are having after school, then it turns to the professional league. The discussion revolves around who is winning the league, who has been traded and the fight in the game that was on television last night. During what the teenagers consider boring activities in class, they invent a form of a hockey game with each other that consists of spinning a coin as a face off and then seeing who can get it in the other's goal, namely off the side of the table. This creates an annoying noise that disturbs others, especially me.

At Sherwood Junior High today, in one class, the students were talkative and I had to send several of them to the office because they were disturbing the class. Then I could hear the sound of the impromptu hockey game. Some teens were not paying attention to the lesson because they were too busy trying to stop the "puck" or coin from going over the edge of the desk. I told the class that if I caught the culprits, I would keep the money. Today I earned my 2 cents worth!

Friday, Nov 17

Talking to parents about their child's misdemeanours can sometimes be a difficult experience. Most parents are fully aware of their child's shortcomings and are receptive to hearing about the problems whether it be homework not done or misbehaviour in class or even fighting. Some, however, are not. They will reply with such terms as, "my son would never do that" or "my daughter was not like that last year. It must be you." These parents undermine the efforts of the teacher to help the child improve in both self-discipline and in his or her educational career. Because of these types of comments, teachers learn to phrase their concerns as tactfully as possible.

I am teaching the same class at Sherwood again today but I didn't earn any coins. It's amazing how students quickly learn what a teacher will tolerate. The classes were wonderful. We watched science videos which we all enjoyed.

At lunch time, the vice-principal came into the staff room. With laughter, he told us how he had approached an issue with a parent. He had said, "I didn't know your son had pierced his penis until he started showing it to the other students."

Monday, Nov 20

Instrumental band is one of my favourite subjects to teach on a temporary basis. Not because I have any talent in this area, but because, at all ages it is an optional subject. Only those who are interested will choose to take instrumental band. By the time they reach junior high, those who have demonstrated some talent will continue with it. Others will drop the course and spend the time in reviewing work or doing another subject such as art. Almost invariably, band students will also be in the top fifty percent of the academic profile as well.

At Meadowbrook Junior High today, I was teaching instrumental band.

Band teachers, like many teachers, do not expect short-term substitutes to teach new work. There is no learning of new keys or practice of difficult passages. In other words, the drudgery of learning to play an instrument is forgotten for the day. The children practice familiar tunes that they have played many times. Sometimes, it can be in the form of a request. At other times, the band teacher dictates what is to be played. Because I don't have enough skill to correct them unless the piece is really awful, it's fun for them and it's fun for me. I only had to conduct, following the lead of the percussionist. It was a great day.

Tuesday, Nov 21

Some extroverted students are able to find appropriate ways to get attention. Even if they don't know a teacher, they will discuss many and sundry topics with the new person. This is because they have been made to feel comfortable in the school setting and trust anyone who is found in that setting. Sometimes they will say more to an adult whom they will only see rarely than to someone they will see every day.

After a quiet weekend, I was back teaching junior high, this time at Sherwood. I knew it would be a fairly difficult day when I went in but the teacher had three preparation periods that day. When a teacher has that many preparation periods in one day, it means there are none on another day. Therefore, one day will be much easier than another since teaching all day with no breaks can be exhausting.

The young teens were their usual selves but Travis asked if he could show me a magic trick. I agreed, hoping it wouldn't disturb the others. He took his left arm out of the sleeve of his sweater. He lifted his empty left sleeve with his right hand and at the same time punched the inside of his sweater with his left hand. It was actually quite funny and I laughed. This, of course, caused an uproar in the class which took a few minutes to settle. I suppose I will never learn.

Later in the day, I had a conversation with a young lady named Erin. Erin told me that her brother was very sick with cancer. She said he was in the hospital and wasn't expected to recover. I didn't know what to say. I asked some questions to get her to talk as much as she wanted to and left a note for her teacher. I knew that I might not see Erin again for a long time so I hope she got some counselling help.

Wednesday, Nov 22

When learning a specialist subject such as French or music, elementary students get to leave the surroundings of their familiar classroom and travel to a new class. They have the opportunity to talk in the halls while walking and become excited in the process. The atmosphere in that new room, then, can be different than the atmosphere of their regular room and the children will act accordingly.

Today I was teaching elementary core French. Since this is only for grades four to six and since there were only two classes of each at one school, the teacher travelled to two schools. She worked mornings at one school and afternoons at another. The next day she switched.

When I started each class I asked, "Do you want to work in French or English?" A substitute has the option of being a little more flexible than the regular teacher.

"English," they shouted and I knew I had won them over for the day.

One class of grade fours was unusually chatty. I said to them, "I thought grade fours were good classes."

One student replied, "We usually are, but this is French!"

Thursday, Nov 23

Students who are developmentally delayed need individual help during the day. Often that help is with a teacher's aide but sometimes they need to be placed in special classes because they simply cannot function within an atmosphere where there are twenty-five to thirty-five other students. Many of these children are happy and enthusiastic and it is usually a delight to work with them.

I taught math and resource at Nottingham today. The math classes were quite enjoyable. Later I went to the resource room where I had one student, Willow.

Willow was sixteen but functioned at a grade two level. She couldn't converse well orally because she also had physical development problems. She usually communicated by writing on a notepad. When I came to the class, she was reading a simple story and she started to read it out loud to me. She had difficulty reading words of more than one syllable but she tried so hard. I could tell right away that Willow had more intelligence than she could speak. I also found out that she had a great sense of humour. When I asked her to point to one of her spelling words, she pointed to all of the words except the correct one. The entire time she was giggling. It was her way of teasing the substitute.

Friday, Nov 24

On special occasions, teachers will show movies to their students. They do their best to choose appropriate films that are rated G for elementary or PG for junior and senior high. Many films of educational quality have higher ratings and, if a teacher wants to show them, a permission form must be signed by the parent. Sometimes, as careful as a teacher is, mishaps will occur, much to the embarrassment of the teacher and the delight of the students.

I was asked to fill in for the guidance counsellor at Nottingham Junior High today. Apparently most of the administrative staff was participating in an activity day and I was placed wherever I was needed. For the first two hours, I was the secretary because the secretary was doing an activity with a couple of classes. I answered phones, looked after the children who were late, and called parents of those who were not feeling well. It was a totally different experience for me.

Next, I had two young men who, because of various indiscretions, were not allowed to participate in the day's activities. They were assigned to clean out a storage room and I was to supervise. They did a lot of work and the room looked much better when they were finished. One of the boys told me he would rather do this than do the other activities that were planned.

After lunch, there was a movie for the school. They watched *My Big Fat Greek Wedding*. At the beginning of the tape there were previews of another movie. Unfortunately for the staff, that movie was rated R and the preview showed a woman wearing a bra. A male staff member jumped in front of the lens to block the image but not before there was a cheer from the boys.

My Big Fat Greek Wedding was enjoyable and the students were very cooperative. Unfortunately, the day finished before the movie. Now I will have to rent it so I can see the ending.

Monday, Nov 27

For teenagers who stay at school for lunch, it is an opportunity to do activities that are not part of the main curriculum. There will be chess clubs, knitting clubs, video clubs, computer clubs, intramural sports, dance and so on. All these extra curricular activities must be supervised by a teacher who volunteers to give up the lunch break in order to spend quality time with the children.

At Ridge Road I was asked to teach English, which is a pleasant change. The students were really cooperative and I should have known that they wanted something. At lunch time, I was asked if I would supervise some girls who wanted to practice a dance routine. I agreed. They wanted some boys to practice with them but only one volunteered. At thirteen or fourteen, boys don't think much of dancing but the girls were eager to show off their steps

The girls got their dance routines from music videos but I don't think they had any idea that the dance they were practising was sexually suggestive. Young teens are sometimes so naïve in their innocence. Even the boy who was practising the routine with them could not see the sexual innuendo in the dance steps. I wonder, when he and his friends get older, if the friends will realize what a missed opportunity they had.

Tuesday, Nov 28

In early elementary, teachers are just recognizing that there are some serious medical problems in the classroom and the children are being tested for them. This is where such diagnoses as autism and dyslexia are made. The earlier these problems are found, the better it is for the student. Early intervention is the key. In fact, now, in many cases, the diagnosis has been made before the child has even entered the school system. Unfortunately, sometimes the diagnosis is missed and help is delayed until much later. In some cases, the parents refuse to accept the advice of the teacher and do not allow their children to be tested. Why? I can only speculate. The only person who suffers in this case is the child who is left to struggle without professional programs and extra assistance.

Today, I was teaching an elementary class, grade one in fact. The students were quite good for the most part but there were a few problems. In this class, two children have been diagnosed with autism. Another child had problems with his eyesight and, even with strong glasses, was unable to see what was written on the board or, indeed, almost anything. It made for an interesting day to say the least. An Educational Program Assistant was assigned to the class to help with these three children; however, it would have been better if they could have had one each. Between the two of us it was all we could do to keep the class running smoothly.

The child with the less severe autism, David, came into the class and by 9:00 had started to throw a temper tantrum because he thought the others in the class were looking at him. Well, I suppose they were. It is hard not to look at someone who is having a temper tantrum. I removed him from the class and put him in a special time-out chair located in the hallway beside the classroom door. After a few minutes the assistant let him come back in and he promptly threw another one. This lasted until lunch time.

Meanwhile, I had twenty other students to teach, each one wanting individual help on their particular assignment. The boy who was almost blind needed almost one-on-one assistance and we did the best to provide it but David was occupying much of our time. Finally, we had to send David to the office because it was becoming much too difficult to teach the class.

After lunch, David came back looking much more relaxed and he had a fairly good afternoon, and so did we, that is until the assistant left for the day. I was left with 21 students who had to pack up their work for the day and put on snowsuits, boots, hats and scarves. About half of them needed help and I was distracted from the full supervision of the autistic students. Just then, there was a commotion at the water fountain.

The second autistic boy, Graham, had found a new game, and as autistic children tend to do, put all his effort into playing it. He was holding down the heads of the grade primary students into the water fountain and forcing them to drink. He would not let them come up to breathe. I grabbed him quickly and forced him away from the fountain. I shudder to think what might have happened if I hadn't noticed the problem when I did. Thank goodness, no one was hurt. It was a scary moment for me.

Wednesday, Nov 29

In inner city schools, course language is an issue, beginning at the senior elementary classroom. Children hear the words "fuck," "asshole," and worse on a regular basis on the street and at home. From the earliest age, children will say the words they hear and these words become part of their vocabulary. Usually every effort is taken by parents and teachers to discourage the use of this type of language and until puberty, children usually listen. After that, the need to express their independence results in the use of coarse language on a regular basis.

I was at the same elementary school today but this time I was teaching grade six. This was an excellent class and had few of the problems of the grade one class of yesterday. In fact, there appeared to be no problems in this class at all. All the children worked hard on their lessons and caused few distractions. Being in an suburban area, the children had not yet heard the vulgar language of the streets on a regular basis and knew that polite society did not condone such language. They did not use it. It was not heard, even accidentally, in the halls. They would have been shocked if they had heard it.

For the last half-hour of the day I was asked to read a chapter or two from a novel that the teacher was reading to the class. Dianne asked if she could read some of it. I read for about fifteen minutes and passed the book on to her. She read one page and looked at me. She came over. I thought she needed help with a word. She pointed and I said, "instructor."

"No," replied Dianne, distressed, "not that word. This one."

I looked at the word "damm".

I read the sentence to her. "That damm instructor."

"I can't say that!" she said.

"It's part of the story. Go up and read it."

Reluctantly she did but not very loudly.

Poor Dianne. I think I shattered some of her illusions today.

Thursday, Nov 30

For some children, the only secure home they have is their school home. They have been placed in one foster home or group home after another. They are not orphans and cannot be adopted but, for one reason or another, their parents cannot look after them. The friendships that they make at school with students and teachers are the only strong ties that they have. They can be quite reluctant to break those bonds.

For the last day of November, I am working at Quaker Grove. One boy, Herb, had just moved from the area to a group home in another part of the city. He had told his social worker that he wanted to stay at Quaker Grove so he could keep his school friends. This is an unusual procedure but both the school administration and the social worker agreed that, in this case, it would be the best for him. Herb had to leave at 6:00 a.m. to take the bus so he would be at school for 9:00. Apparently, he was seldom late. At lunch time Herb told me he was really hungry but he had already eaten his lunch. I gave him the money to buy a bag of chips. Herb promised to repay me but I didn't expect him to. Yet, the next time I was at Quaker Grove, Herb had the money waiting.

DECEMBER

Friday, Dec 1

Advent has started. The three weeks before Christmas can be a very trying time for teachers. The junior high students are far more excited about Christmas than the primary grades. Even senior high students will get into the Christmas spirit early. All students find it hard to contain their emotions and concentrate on school work.

I was back at Sunnybrae High this afternoon. Unfortunately, there wasn't much work left by the teacher to occupy them. To be fair, I know it's difficult, sometimes, to find the correct amount of work. Teachers don't want to start new work if they have a substitute because the children may claim that the substitute taught the wrong thing, or they may claim that the substitute didn't know how to teach and they didn't understand. Teenagers will make any excuse for not learning the work except putting the blame on themselves because they wanted to have fun that period. Often, to a teenager, a substitute means time off.

When they had finished their work, some of the boys played with finger skate boards. I thought, "Small minds enjoy small things." This isn't really fair, though, because these are the students who had completed all the assigned work. Boys (even though they are 6'3") will be boys.

Monday, Dec 4

A teacher must be very careful what he or she says to a class, especially during the Christmas season. Even some twelve- and thirteen-year-olds still believe in the existence of Santa Claus, especially when Christmas approaches and any remark to the contrary will bring controversy or, at the least, discussion.

It's the start of a new week and now we're really into the advent season. I was teaching at Sherwood Junior High, grade eight English. As usual, grade eights were a little more of a problem than the other classes. They did their work but I made the near-fatal mistake. I mentioned Santa Claus. This caused an argument between two students.

"Santa Claus doesn't exist."

"Yes, he does. He may not bring presents when we're older but there is a Santa Claus."

"No there isn't. Our parents bring the gifts. There is no Santa Claus."

"Yes there is. Santa Claus is like God. We can't see him but he is there."

This argument was getting too deep for me so I steered the class back to their work.

NOTE TO SELF: Don't mention Santa Claus in class again.

Tuesday, Dec 5

Another controversy in the classroom is the subject of religion. Most people in Canada believe in the separation of church and state. Yet, there are many Canadians who attend religious ceremonies on a regular basis. Even "O Canada" which, as a rule, is sung in schools on a daily basis, mentions God. There are many children have no more knowledge of God than this. How can we understand the culture of the religious citizens of our own country if we neglect our children's religious education?

In many countries, there is no separation of church and state. Politics is based not on secular ideas but on religion and this has the support of most of that country's citizens. How can we understand the culture of these countries if we're kept in ignorance of the most important part of their lives?

I was teaching at Meadowbrook Junior High today. The classes, as usual, were excellent. I really like teaching at a technically advanced school. The students were working on projects and all I had to do was make sure they were on track and keep an eye out for computer games, chatting, and inappropriate web sites and so on. There were no real problems.

One of the projects in a grade nine class was to write an essay on the commercialism of Christmas. I was reading over Roddy's shoulder. He was writing that Christmas was his favourite holiday because he got presents. He paused in his typing, looked at me and asked, "Why do we have Christmas anyway?"

I pointed to the part of the word—Christ.

"Christ," he said, "is he a God or something?"

At first I thought he was making fun of me or was trying to cause a disturbance. Then I realized that he really didn't know. He said he had never been taken to any religious event, Christian or otherwise. I then explained to him the story of Christmas and why Christians hold the celebration on December twenty-fifth every year.

Wednesday, Dec 6

The weather can play havoc with the best laid plans. When the roads are dangerous because of weather conditions, it is better to err on the side of caution and pull school busses off the road. Although there are parents who complain because they have to find babysitters or take time off work to stay home to look after their children, it is far better that their children are safe than that there is a major accident where one or more of those children are seriously injured or killed.

It's a partial snow day today and although school isn't cancelled the busses are. I was teaching at Meadowbrook Junior High and ninety percent of the students are bus students. That means that there are only about fifteen percent of the students in the school. No, my math isn't wrong. Some parents will drive their children to school if the busses are cancelled.

Unfortunately, the children who do come to school are usually the top students who don't need any remedial help. It's impossible to teach new material because most of the students are absent.

Another grade seven class combined with mine and we watched a *Harry Potter* movie. Even though I had already seen it, I enjoyed it as did the children.

In the afternoon, we worked on Christmas decorations. As in most schools, there was a best-decorated-class contest and grade seven students are always eager to participate. All I did was supply the materials and these great kids did wonders with the classroom. What fun.

Thursday, Dec 7

It seems that no matter how polite, responsible and intelligent the child, when they reach thirteen, rebelliousness will replace those positive characteristics. Fortunately, this period only lasts for a year or two. Unfortunately, in the classroom, it seems to become more pronounced in girls.

Today I returned to Meadowbrook to teach instrumental band. They had a concert that evening and I was to do the dress rehearsal. I wasn't sure I was up to that but, as always, I did my best.

We rehearsed in the gym. They were reasonably good for the

most part. All I had to do was keep time. The percussion section was excellent, so I just followed them. The grade eights were their usual selves. They just would not rehearse properly. They would not pay attention to the music. They would talk among themselves and not come in on time. They wouldn't even listen to instructions and played the wrong song. I did my best but the children didn't do theirs.

At the end of the rehearsal, I reminded the class that they had to be at the school at 6:30 for the concert at 7:00.

"What!" exclaimed Rosie. "When are we going to have the dress rehearsal?"

"You just had it," I replied.

There wasn't a happy look on her face. She well knew that she was so busy trying to frustrate the substitute that she didn't rehearse.

There is a saying that if the dress rehearsal is bad, the performance will be good. By all accounts, it was.

Friday, Dec 8

At Christmas time, many elementary schools have some type of presentation. At some schools it is a holiday concert, at others it is a variety show and at others there is a play. No matter what the presentation, many hours are spent in rehearsal by both teachers and students. The students themselves are most excited and do their best to be the star of the show. Even the primary child who plays the part of a flower is convinced that she is the best in the show. Parents and teachers are quick to reassure her that she was.

The children in a grade four class were excited. They were putting on a performance of *Narnia* tonight. Although they didn't have any of the staring rolls because these were reserved for the grade six class, many of the children had roles that they felt were crucial to the performance. The dress rehearsal was in the afternoon.

The play was excellent. I was surprised at how such young children can memorize so many lines. Some of them were outstanding actors and the scenery was breathtaking. Apparently a parent, who is also an artist, did all the decorations. The backdrop of the field of flowers was amazing.

After the play, the grade fours came back into the class. "How was I?" each one asked in turn.

Since they were in costume as squirrels, birds, deer, and bears I had no idea who played what part. "Great. Wonderful," I replied. All they did was run across the stage on two occasions, but, indeed, all of them were wonderful.

Monday, Dec 11

Sometimes, because of size, a school is unable to use their facilities for their presentation. In this case, they will rent or borrow the facilities from another school, usually a high school. Most high schools have a group of students who are trained to run the sound system.

At another elementary school today, I was asked to teach grade six. In the morning, the school went to Kennedy High for a concert rehearsal. Unfortunately, the sound system was not working properly. We sat in the gym for an hour while the high school students tried to fix the system. The children, naturally, were bored and quite noisy during this time. Amazingly, as soon as the sound system started to work, they became quiet. No one had to say anything to them. They knew exactly what to do and did it. The rehearsal went very well and I enjoyed it immensely.

Tuesday, Dec 12

Keeping the belief in Santa Claus alive in junior high can be to a teacher's advantage, especially if that teacher is a substitute and has a round face, greying hair and glasses. This is especially true if she is wearing a red dress with a green sweater. Although it was not my intention to look a little like Mrs. Claus, apparently at this time of year, I do.

Today, I went to Parkview Junior High to teach grade seven. Most of the students were wonderful as usual but one student, Irene, was a little disruptive. Wanda became impatient and said, "Irene, please be quiet!"

A few minutes later, Irene was sitting on the back of a chair. I said to her, "Irene, please sit properly."

"How did you know my name?" she asked, forgetting that someone had mentioned her name earlier.

I looked at her over the top of my glasses and said, "I'm like Santa Claus. I know everything!"

"Are you Mrs. Claus?"

"You never know," I replied. Irene was very good for the rest of the class but I noticed that, every once in a while, she peeked up to make sure I was watching her being good.

Wednesday, Dec 13

When a cold or the flu hits a school it quickly spreads to all students and staff. Sometimes it seems that everyone in the building is in one stage or another of the illness. This can cause havoc with the best laid plans, especially when the absenteeism rate is high.

I was asked to teach French immersion at Parkview where the flu bug had taken hold. Along with the teacher who was sick, one-third of the class was absent. In addition, another one-third seemed to either be starting to get sick or who were returning from being sick. I tried to avoid the coughers but it wasn't easy. There was always someone asking to go to the washroom to blow a nose. "Est-ce que J'allés au toilette?" was a common question that day.

Thursday, Dec 14

The Quaker Grove administration does its best to help their students without giving the impression that they are providing charity. They had set up a lost and found room, which all schools have. The difference in the lost and found room at Quaker Grove is that it held clean and tidy used clothes that had been donated by various groups and schools. The children at the school didn't know this. They thought they were clothes that had gone unclaimed at their own school.

I was teaching grade three today. Of all the grades, I think this is the one that teachers love the most. At this age, they are accustomed to the routine of school. They know that they must put their hand up to ask a question. They know that they must ask permission to get a book from the back or leave a class and so on. They can read quite well and are eager to learn new vocabulary. They are still curious about the world and every lesson gives them something new to think about. They are eager to please and simply adore their teacher. No one has started the first transition into puberty.

This grade three is no different. They were helpful, cooperative and eager to do the assigned work. During the afternoon, they were asked to go to the lost and found room to see if they owned any of the clothes that were there. When they arrived, they were encouraged to take anything they could use. Arlene returned and said to me, "You should see all the clothes in the lost and found! I was able to get my brother's Christmas present. I got boots, jeans and a sweater. He will be so excited!"

He probably will not be as excited as Arlene was to be able to give her brother a gift.

Friday, Dec 15

By law, a person who is not licensed to teach must be supervised when teaching or presenting a lesson in the classroom.

Therefore, when a student teacher is in the classroom, she must be supervised. The supervisor does not necessarily have to be in the same room but must be nearby.

This morning I woke up with a sore throat. Obviously, I didn't avoid all the coughers on Wednesday. I was asked to teach at Meadowbrook Junior High today. I was pleased with this assignment because it should prove to be a good day, even with the cold.

When I left home, the temperature was above freezing and there was no precipitation. About fifteen minutes later, I reached the Parkview area and there was about five cm. of snow on the road. Traffic was almost at a standstill. What should have been a thirty-minute drive took forty-five minutes and I was late. I only had a few minutes to get ready for the day. With the sore throat, I was not sure I could cope.

When I arrived, I was told I had a student teacher to help with the class. Actually, as it turned out, the student teacher did most of the teaching. I had to be there in case there were problems but, with the bug I had caught, I was pleased that I could sit most of the day.

Sadly, I had outdoor lunch duty that day and I had to go outside in the snowstorm. I had no boots, no hat or gloves. I wore only a spring coat.

NOTE TO SELF: Remember to listen to the weather forecast before leaving in the morning.

TGIF. I had all weekend to get better.

Monday, Dec 18

This is the last week before Christmas break and it proved to be a good one.

I was at Meadowbrook Junior High teaching instrumental band until the Christmas Break. What a wonderful opportunity. I didn't have to fight the Christmas excitement that will be in the other classes. Since the students only had band twice in a six-day cycle, I was teaching the same lessons over and over. Therefore, there wasn't a lot of preparation to do either.

Today, I saw grade eights. As usual the grade eights needed to be kept busy to avoid problems and the teacher wisely chose a great lesson. We listened to the "Nutcracker Suite" while the children drew pictures to illustrate each scene. Many of them had gone to the ballet as part of a family Christmas tradition and were familiar with the music and the story. The children enjoyed the music and the pictures were impressive. It was a wonderful day to be a teacher.

Tuesday, Dec 19

Children must realize that the only way to improve their skill in any area, whether it is sports, music or math, is practice and practice and more practice. Nevertheless, practising an instrument can be as tedious as doing homework and children have to be reminded that practice is the key to success. Part of being a band teacher, then, is allowing children the opportunity to practice whenever possible.

During this week, the grade nine students were watching a movie about the importance of practice, starring Yo Yo Ma, the cellist. The children were especially interested in his techniques and his subsequent successes. They were respectful, pleasant and helpful.

At lunch time, a rock band wanted to practice. Although I knew it would probably hurt my sensitive ears, I said yes. The children were so serious. They were going to be the next big superstars. They have a long, long way to go. As far as I could tell, they only knew one song which they played over and over and over and over again.

As I searched for a pain reliever for my headache, I reminded myself that, indeed, practice does make perfect.

Wednesday, Dec 20

Children get confused when it comes to the relationships of adults. If a male and female teacher of the same last name are in a school, they automatically assume they are married. This might be true but most of the time there is no relationship. At the same time, two teachers who are friendly may be considered to have a romantic relationship and rumours abound. In some cases it is fun to laugh at the assumptions but at other times it can become downright embarrassing.

Yesterday, Lois, a student, asked me if I was married to Mr. Doyle. I said yes and there was a stir of excitement. Now there is a rumour that I am married to the physical education teacher who has the same last name as mine, whom, by the way, I had never met.

Lois clarified my answer to yesterday's question. "Is your husband a teacher?"

"No," I replied.

"But you said you were married to Mr. Doyle."

"I am. My name is Mrs. Doyle and my husband's name is Mr. Doyle."

"That's not what I meant when I asked if you were married to Mr. Doyle. I meant Mr. Doyle, the phys. ed. teacher."

Grinning, I replied, "That's not what you said."

Thursday, Dec 21

To most junior high students, giving Christmas presents is as much or more important as receiving them. This was the last day of school before Christmas Vacation and the children were in a highly excitable state. They came to school with presents for friends and teachers, and they were going from class to class to distribute them. Although most of the children in this school are from middle to upper-middle socio-economic families, they were very pleased with the presents from their friends that were worth only a dollar or two. Indeed, it is the thought that counts and these children demonstrated it well.

Several gifts were given to me to give to the regular band teacher. I made sure they would be delivered. Then there was a surprise. Travis, of the rock band fame, came to the door and gave me a sun catcher which said "World's Greatest Music Teacher."

"I'll make sure your regular teacher gets this," I said, thanking him.

"No, it's for you." Travis smiled.

"For me?" I exclaimed. "Surely, you bought it for your teacher."

"No," he assured me, "it's for you."

I was flattered and flustered at the same time. I didn't expect a gift. After all I had only been in the class for five days. "Thank you very much," I said.

I definitely am not a music teacher. I cannot sing at all and I have very little music ability but Travis must have seen something somewhere. It will be a gift I'll treasure for the rest of my life.

JANUARY

Wednesday, Jan 3

Origami has become a popular craft with both adults and children. When I was in school, the only type of paper folding that we did consisted of turning a piece of paper into the shape of a small square that had flaps at the corners. A game would be played where each corner of the square would be opened in turn and a funny or rude saying would be written under the opening. Needless to say, these were banned in the classroom.

After a nice long Christmas break, I went back to work teaching junior high at Ridge Road where the grade sevens were starting to get comfortable in their new environment and the puberty hormones were beginning to rage. In other words, it wouldn't be long before the grade sevens would be starting to behave like grade eights.

Over the Christmas break, someone had learned the game of yesteryear. Probably a grandmother has taught her grandchildren the game we used to play. They played this game with each other causing much hilarity and, of course, disturbance of their lessons. I had to confiscate several of them during the course of the day.

Thursday, Jan 4

In most schools, parents and students are responsible for raising their own money for a school trip, but at Quaker Grove most of the parents had no extra money or time. Since no one wanted the children to have fewer opportunities than those in more affluent neighbourhoods, the school and its teachers assumed the responsibility for raising money.

Today, at Quaker Grove Junior High, I was teaching core French. I did the best I could but the morning was one of the more difficult ones.

In the afternoon, the grade nine class was making covered coat hangers to sell to raise money for a trip. Although I do many crafts at home, I had never done this particular one and many of the children needed help with this craft as well. Michelle, an especially responsible student, was a natural. She became the teacher and I became the student. Michelle helped the others with the craft and taught me how to do it. I was able to cover two hangers which I gave to Michelle as a thank you. She would sell these to raise money for herself.

Friday, Jan 5

In a small high school, all the students know each other. Since there are fewer teachers, the children become quite familiar with their instructors and everyone enjoys the friendly environment. This is certainly true at Kennedy High.

Students were quietly reading *Wuthering Heights* when a young man popped his head around the door. "Can I help you?"

"I'm just looking for some lovely ladies," Dale replied.

"Well, you found one," I quipped. Dale laughed and left.

Ivan said to me, "You're hot."

Lindy added, "Do you know what that means?"

Thinking that the meaning of the phrase must have changed since I had last heard it I answered in the negative.

"You're blushing," Ivan pointed out. Everyone laughed so I

suppose the phrase still means what it used to and I enjoyed the ego boost.

Monday, Jan 8

The months between Christmas and March Break are difficult. It is winter with all that it entails. There are no statutory holidays between Christmas and March Break in my part of Canada so the only breaks the children get are for teacher in-servicing and storm days. By mid February, it seems that winter will never end, March will never come and the children get tired of studying. This becomes difficult on teachers as well because they are trying so hard to motivate their students.

At the beginning of this long haul, I was asked to teach grade eight core French and math at Ridge Road. The math was fun because I rarely have a class in my subject area so I enjoy it when I do. We were studying exponents so I looked forward to some good days.

In core French, the students would be watching *Le Seigneur des Anneaux* or *The Lord of the Rings*. The entire dialogue would be in French. Since I am teaching six grade eight classes, by the end of the week, I would have watched it six times—all in French.

Tuesday, Jan 9

Children, as a rule, enjoy watching movies when they are presented as an educational tool. However, if the movie is above their skill level, they will become frustrated and will not be able to concentrate on it leading to behaviour problems.

The math went well. I had some talkative students, but grade eight is grade eight and it is difficult to expect much more. Most of the time, the children stopped talking and did their work. Hopefully, they appreciated my skill in math and my ability to help them.

The French was driving me crazy. Watching *Le Seigneur des Anneaux* over and over became exasperating. Each class had only one and one-half hours of French per a six-day cycle. For the one-half hour class, by the time they arrived and got settled, there was only twenty to twenty-five minutes of actual viewing. For the hour class there was more. However, during this week, I won't see the video in its entirety but I did see the same clip over and over again. I became frustrated.

Wednesday, Jan 10

When DVD's became popular, it helped in scene selection. It became much easier to choose where to start a movie. However, Ridge Road didn't have a DVD player at this time and the VHS format had to be used. Since the counter did not work properly on the VCR I had to remember exactly where each class started and stopped.

I had to rewind the tape over and over again. Being grade eights, the students had little patience for my mistakes. If I had it set for the wrong place for a particular class, the students got restless, complained and I had difficulty getting them settled for the class. Most of the time, I got it right. I started each class just before they finished the previous day so they could review the scene. Those with good memories objected but it worked well for the most part.

By the time I had seen a scene for the sixth time in French, I could almost understand the dialog. Since I have far more experience in speaking and understanding French than the grade eights, I wondered how these emerging French students were doing. I had also seen the English version and read the book so I understood the plot. Those who have not seen the English version must have found the movie tremendously confusing.

Thursday, Jan 11

The students were starting to get used to me in the classroom. There were far fewer problems than I had when I first started. The talkers in math were settling down and doing their work. They were asking questions and understanding my answers. I was getting control and loving my job.

Today I was told that I would be at Ridge Road for another week. Great! That means that I would be able to watch all of *Le Seigneur des Anneaux*—six times!

Some of the boys, however, were still challenging my rules. One rule, standard in most schools, was that only one person could leave the classroom at a time. Lloyd came up to my desk and started jumping up and down. This is a common sign that boys will use to show they are in urgent need. "Can I go to the bathroom?" asked Lloyd. I answered in the negative because another student had asked only moments before.

The jumping became more vigorous and his voice became louder. "I have to go, I'm on my period!" Apparently Lloyd thought that if this worked with the girls it should also work for him.

Friday, Jan 12

As a substitute teacher, it is not my place to change or adapt the school policy. Sometimes, however, in the absence of administrative guidance, it seems that that is exactly what must be done. At such times, I use my own judgement and hope that I do not get into too much trouble for taking things into my own hands.

The weather had become exceedingly cold. There was a temperature of -17° C with a wind chill of -30° C. My favourite place on days like this is in front of the fireplace with a hot chocolate in my hand. However, that will be tomorrow's agenda.

Today I was on duty in the morning. I was determined not to go outside! Administrators had not yet arrived for the day so I made the choice. I was just not going to let myself or the children freeze. I let the children into the lobby of the school and supervised them there. No one said anything to me about it so I must have been right.

Monday, Jan 15

Young teens like to push the limits but they are fully aware of what the limits should be and they respect anyone that keeps them on the straight and narrow; even though they are loathe to admit it.

The grade eights were starting to relate to me. I was getting hugs when they entered the classroom. I was told that I was the only teacher who could keep them in line. In one class a group of boys started chanting, "Doyle rules. Doyle rules." At times like this I feel that this job is worthwhile. I will miss then when I leave.

Tuesday, Jan 16

Some children use misbehaviour to mask their frustration in doing a lesson. When they misbehave enough, they earn the privilege of being asked to leave the class. On some occasions they even get sent home where they can forget about the lesson. In other cases, the children know that any misbehaviour will result in severe sanctions at home and will not resort to that. However, some of these children will develop a great sense of humour. If they can get the teacher laughing, they take the pressure off themselves.

Kevin was one of the children who found math difficult. As I walked around the room, checking their ability to do the day's math lesson, I asked Kevin, "How are you making out?"

"Actually, I am not making out at all," he replied with a grin. NOTE TO SELF: Don't use that phrase again.

Wednesday, Jan 17

We had almost finished watching *Le Seigneur des Anneaux*. I had now seen it six times in French and once in English. I don't think I will watch it again for a long, long time. I had almost memorized the scenes. Yet, every time I saw it, I saw something I missed the previous time. Again, though, I wondered how much the grade eight core French classes were getting out of it. After all, they were only seeing it once and in a foreign language.

Kevin was working slowly in math. When I passed his desk I encouraged him to work a little faster. The third time he asked, "Do you have any horses?"

I must have looked puzzled because he grinned at me. Then I understood. "No, I don't have any horses to hold today." I wish he was as sharp at math.

Thursday, Jan 18

At least once a year, the administration will offer a production to the entire student body. These concerts are not only entertaining but also include inspirational encouragement and lessons about drug and alcohol abuse, violence, peer pressure, bullying and so on. Some of the presenters are tremendously gifted individuals who have become famous in their own right.

In math, I had switched to teaching algebra. I knew it was the first time these classes have been exposed to algebraic equations so I tried to explain it as carefully as I could. I repeated the lesson many different ways. Several, including Kevin, said that this type of math was fun.

In the afternoon, there was an inspirational concert put on by a local singer. I and my classes enjoyed the break. It was nice to get away from *Le Seigneur des Anneaux* for a little while.

Friday, Jan 19

The last day of any assignment can be problematic. I was sad to be leaving and so my emotions could get the better of me. The students, who have gotten to know me, had mixed emotions. Some of them were sad that the teacher, whom they had for several weeks, was leaving. Others were excited that the teacher they had since the beginning of the year was returning. Some of the children experienced both emotions at the same time. Combining these feelings with the natural processes of a thirteen-year-old and the influences of a full moon can produce chaos in a classroom.

The math classes were excellent but the core French was a different matter. I had to give several detentions for behaviour and had to inform several parents about the behaviour of their children. Nevertheless, I would miss this group of children. I had fallen in love, as usual.

Monday, Jan 22

They say money doesn't buy happiness, and I suppose they (whoever they are) must be right. I certainly don't substitute teach for the money since I could make much more in another profession, so I must decide what happiness means. If happiness means spending the day with children, as it does for me, then I am happy indeed. If happiness means having an unexpected day to rest then today I am blissful.

School was cancelled and I supposed it was for the best but there went the dollars again. It was too cold to allow children to walk to school. It's -23° C with a wind chill of -40° C. According to the weather forecast, it was the coldest it has been in this area since the 1890s. There wasn't anything to do but put on a fire in the fireplace, cuddle up with a hot chocolate, and catch up on my reading. Indeed, money doesn't buy happiness.

Tuesday, Jan 23

A professional junior hockey team studies at Dover High. Exceptions are made for practices and game days when the boys are absent from class. It's a difficult job to play hockey full time and attend school full time, but sixteen- to eighteen-year-olds have lots of energy and most are able to do it successfully.

Having a professional hockey team in a school provides perks to the other students and teachers. There are often free tickets to the games and, of course, a person can always say I knew that famous player when he was going to school.

In family studies, some of the students, who were young mothers, were allowed to bring their babies and toddlers to class for the day. One little boy was with his mother as I passed in the hallway. There were a couple of hockey players nearby.

"Hi, little one," I said. "Do you like hockey?"

His eyes lit up when he replied, "Oh, yes!"

"Let me introduce you to two people who play for the local professional team," I said.

"Oh…" he said, hesitantly, "I really don't like that team."

I suppose sixteen- and seventeen-year-old pro hockey players need their egos deflated occasionally!

Wednesday, Jan 24

Hats are forbidden in many schools. It is one of the rules that is strictly enforced. One reason is that it's considered impolite to wear headwear indoors. For another, and perhaps more important, students, similar to ostriches, like to hide in their hoods so you can't see the expressions on their faces. If I can't see you, then you can't see me!

I returned to the same school as yesterday. Alex arrived in the classroom with the hood of his sweatshirt pulled over his head. Three times, a magic number it seems, I asked him to remove his hood. Finally he complied but as soon as he did, he lightly punched another student. I asked him to sit in another seat. He refused. Alex was starting to escalate the situation so, for the safety of the other students, it was time to remove him from the class.

I gave Alex the choice to change seats or go to the office. Alex threatened to throw his desk. I called his bluff and he raised his desk over his head. Finally and thankfully Alex decided that he had crossed over the line and went to the office. Alex got three days suspension simply because he tried to push the rule of wearing headgear in the classroom.

Thursday, Jan 25

Students with Down's syndrome are a pleasure to teach. They are always cheerful and appreciate all the help that they are given. They almost never cause behaviour problems and usually obey instructions. However, like everyone else, they can be stubborn at times and will follow their own inclinations.

James, at Parkview Junior, suffered from Down's syndrome. He was a very nice young man with quite a sense of humour. The class was studying First Nations history and was discussing the flora and fauna of British Columbia. James was having difficulty understanding the questions and providing answers.

"James," I asked, "what kinds of plants grow in the forests of British Columbia?"

"Marijuana," he replied with a grin. I supposed that James must watch the nightly news.

"You are right; someone has probably planted some there," I said, "but what other plants would there be?

"Trees, flowers," he answered and wrote that in his notebook.

Then I asked, "James, what kind of animals live in the forest?"

With a twinkle in his eye, he replied, "Elves." Perhaps he had seen *Lord of the Rings*.

"Elves?" I questioned. "No, not elves. What else?"

"Deer, bears," he said.

"Good, now write that in your notebook."

James wrote deer, bears and he grinned at me. I looked at his work. Underneath deer and bears, he had written elves.

Friday, Jan 26

Adolescent boys grow at different rates. In grade eight it is not unusual to see one fourteen-year-old boy who is six feet tall and another who has not yet reached five feet. It can be emotionally stressful for the short boy at that age. He cannot compete equally in physical education. He is teased or bullied by his classmates and called "shorty" or some other derogatory name. They don't apply the same type of offensive nicknames to the tall boy. The tall boy is considered somewhat of a hero, simply because he started his teenage growth spurt before the others.

At Dover High I was asked to teach grade eleven and twelve math. They were being tested and I had nothing to do but supervise the tests. This was a boring day but the students were glad that there was someone who could help if they needed it.

As I was standing in the hallway between classes, I noticed two friends walking down the hall engrossed in conversation. One of the boys had to duck to get into the classroom. He must have been close to seven feet tall. His leggy build added to the effect of great height. His best friend was no more than five foot two. I was reminded of the cartoon "Mutt and Jeff."

Monday, Jan 29

At this time of year, a phys. ed. skiing trip is usually planned. Most of the students participate in the trip and are accompanied by some of their teachers but attending the ski trip is a privilege, however, and students who have proved that they cannot be trusted to be responsible on the ski hill will not be allowed to attend. Others will choose not to attend because they don't like to ski, cannot provide the fees required or because of physical difficulties. Because these students are required to be in school, a substitute is hired to replace the teachers who are skiing.

Today, my job at Ridge Road was to replace the grade seven teacher who was skiing. Most of the grade sevens and one-half of the grade nines went on the ski trip. The grade eights were not given the opportunity because of their behaviour problems. In grade seven, I had only four students to supervise. The teacher left some math review exercises for them and I did crossword puzzles. What a great day!

Tuesday, Jan 30

Junior high students, in the heat of the moment, will sometimes act inappropriately. One of the major rules in any school is in regards to the treatment of teachers. It is absolutely forbidden to assault a teacher in any way. This doesn't mean that teachers are never assaulted. Unfortunately, that happens all too often. What it does mean is that there are severe consequences if it happens.

Today, at Mill Cove Consolidated, the situation was much worse than yesterday. At the beginning of the class, Gaston, from grade seven, who was on his way to another classroom, poked his head around the door. I went over to the door, closed it, and rested my hand on the knob while settling the class. Harley suddenly got out of his seat, grabbed my hand and the knob and twisted my hand. He used the door to push me out of the way. Harley was angry and I had no idea why. I sent both Harley and Gaston to the office but they refused to go.

I called Harley's mom and she insisted that Harley would not hurt a teacher. I informed her that indeed he had done so and she was called in to a meeting regarding the incident.

During the meeting, the apparent cause of the minor altercation became apparent. It seemed that Harley and Gaston had gotten into an argument previously. The cause of the argument—what else?—a girl.

Wednesday, Jan 31

Some of the students at Ridge Road are from the black community. Those who are from low-income households feel they are living in a ghetto-like neighbourhood which is far from the truth. There are no ghettos in my area and there will never be. In order for the children to really understand what a ghetto is and what growing up in a ghetto is like, a motivational speaker was brought in.

Lesra Martin grew up in the ghettos of New York. He was found by two Canadians who took him to Toronto to be educated where he eventually became a lawyer and moved to Kamloops. Lesra took on the case of Hurricane Carter who was a black American boxer put in jail for three murders he didn't commit. The case became famous, a movie was made of it and Hurricane Carter was eventually freed.

The students were enthralled. Lesra spoke for about one and one-half hours. Much of the talk was about growing up black in New York and about the terrible schooling the blacks in his home community had had to put up with. Lesra was probably one of the best speakers I have heard and the students asked many questions. The assembly lasted for the entire morning and I had to remind myself that I was actually getting paid for this day.

FEBRUARY

Thursday, Feb 1

Children do not always understand the many dangers that are in our lives and so we must protect our children as much as possible. Sometimes this is not always possible but most parents and teachers do their best.

Today I was teaching a primary class at Quaker Grove. The children were delightful but totally unaware of the environment around them. As they lined up for recess, I checked for zippers, scarves, mittens, hats and boots. One child, Nathan, did not have his jacket zipped up. He was not wearing any mittens or a hat. I looked more closely. He did not have any snow pants on either. As it had snowed the night before, I knew the children would be out building snowmen during the break.

I questioned Nathan about his attire. "Nathan, where is your hat."

"I forgot it."

"Where are you mittens?"

"At home."

"Well, at least put your snow pants on. You can't play in the snow without them. You'll be soaking wet for the rest of the morning. That's how we get sick."

"I'm too big to wear snow pants."

Looking around at the rest of the children, I noticed some of the grade sixes with snow pants. Nathan was half their size and probably only six years old.

I told Nathan to go back into the classroom. He could not go out for recess with the others.

I sent a note home, hoping that Nathan had learned his lesson and would bring the correct attire for the following day.

When they lined up for lunch, Nathan did not even have the zipper of his jacket done up. "I live nearby so I don't have to do it up." No lesson learned there.

When he came back in the afternoon, he still did not have hat, mittens or the zipper done up. Perhaps he will learn his lesson when he gets frostbite on his ears while playing in the snow.

Friday, Feb 2

At the end of first term, all teachers are given a day to prepare their report cards. For most teachers, the preparation usually takes two to three days so this gives them a chance to get started. The rest of the report card preparation is done on the weekend. One of the perks of being a substitute teacher is that I have no report cards to do. Therefore, I have the day off, without pay of course.

Monday, Feb 5

At the age of seven and eight, children need to understand consequences of their behaviour immediately. If they have behaved well, praise should be forthcoming without delay. If they have behaved badly, then the consequences of that behaviour should also be given without ado. Children at this age quickly forget what they have done and why they are receiving consequences for whatever behaviour occurred. Giving detentions after school for something that occurred at 9:00 in the morning just doesn't work.

At this age, also, children will quickly forgive and forget. If they were reprimanded for something that happened an hour ago, then it is over and they start the rest of the day afresh.

For a change I am teaching grade two. What cute children and what disobedient children they are. A new teacher in the classroom has excited them, but at the same time, some of them are a little scared. As soon as they saw me, three children rushed to hide under the teacher's desk. I had to get help to remove them. They went to the office for a time out for half an hour and when they came back they gave me a hug. All was forgotten and forgiven, no grudges were held. The rest of the day was great.

Tuesday, Feb 6

Jumping from junior elementary to high school can cause difficulties in my attitude towards the children. Am I treating the grade twelve students like they were in grade two? Am I treating the grade two students like they were in junior high? There seems to be one commonality with all classes, though. Whenever I am teaching new students, I have three phrases that I always seem to use: "Please sit down quietly," "Please stop talking," and "Let's get to work quickly."

Today I was back teaching high school. I went to Parkview High where the classes were still in split shift with Sunnybrae. Parkview is the one that starts at 7:00 in the morning. As I have mentioned, I'm definitely not a morning person and by the time I and the students woke up, I realized that I was teaching grades ten and twelve math. This proved to be a perfect day. I was able to help the children with their math sheets and they appreciated the help. I was finished by 12:30 and had the rest of the day to myself.

Wednesday, Feb 7

French immersion students, by definition, are usually the best students in the school. However, if a substitute wants to have a great day with these children, it is paramount to give them a little rest from the pressures of speaking in a second language all day long. Sometimes this is easy to accomplish, even if the substitute only knows a little French.

I am in a French immersion class today at the techie school, Meadowbrook Junior High. Again this proved to be a wonderful day, the second in a row.

I started the day by saying, "Bonjour."

There was a collective groan from the students.

Rebecca asked, "Do you speak French?"

"Oui, un petit peu," I replied.

Rebecca said, "Can you speak English, please?"

"OK, just don't tell your teacher."

They promised they would keep it between us and cheered. I had no intention of speaking French all class and I'm sure that their teacher didn't expect me to. However, the students didn't know that and they worked hard for me for the day.

Thursday, Feb 8

Children who live in the inner city are far more streetwise than children who live in the suburbs or in the country. Inner-city children are exposed to more traffic, crime and drug problems. Sometimes these problems reach into their households and affect them personally. Country children, although exposed to these evils, are less likely to know as much about them as their inner-city counterparts. As a result, country children are less cynical about life and therefore more mannerly and more respectful of authority.

I was filling in for a guidance counsellor at Parkview Junior High. She taught two classes of Personal Development and Relationships so they had to get a substitute for her. Parkview Junior High is a school located close to the country so the children are less worldly and more respectful. It was a pleasure to teach at this school.

Other than the two classes I taught, I spent the day in the referral room. This is the room that the students, who have been sent from class for a minor discretion, will stay until the class is over. It seems that schools that have this type of referral room tend to have much better control over their students.

Friday, Feb 9

Because of the restrictions on class sizes, some classes have to be split up. Sometimes it will be a grade one-two class or a two-three class or so on. Split classes are usually found in elementary schools. It is very rare for a secondary teacher to have a split class. Because a teacher must divide her time between the two levels, the children who are placed in a split class are usually the more independent workers. They are the ones who do not need to be reminded to sit quietly, stop talking and get to work.

Today, I am doing a split five-six class. Some of the children in this class were not as independent at working as they should have been. They were up and down, in and out and they talked nonstop. It was a strenuous day, but at the same time, the children were fun. That is, they were fun when I wasn't trying to teach a lesson to them. I was exhausted when the day was over. TGIF

Monday, Feb 12

It's the middle of winter and the middle of the winter blues and the children are getting tired of going to school every day and of the cold weather. They, like the rest of us, need a break. Unfortunately, that isn't going to happen for another month. Because a month seems so far away, the students start getting restless and finding ways to relieve their stresses and boredom.

Today's class at Mill Cove was really difficult. The students had no intention of obeying the lowly substitute. Like yesterday's class, they were up and down in their seats and in and out of the room. When I tried to tell them to stay in class, they argued with me. For the first time this year, I had to get the vice-principal into the room to calm the teenagers down. Fortunately, they did listen, and after a while, I was able to conduct a fairly good lesson.

Tuesday, Feb 13

Group discussions with teenagers can be one of the most challenging lessons a teacher can plan. Students have a lot to say and they tend to blurt out their opinions whenever they happen to think of them. They often have to be reminded that only one person speaks at a time. Teachers sometimes use the First Nation's practice of having a talking stick which works very well. The person holding the stick is the only one allowed to talk. Actually, it does not have to be a stick, it can be a teddy bear, a book or anything else that is available.

It was a relief to be teaching grade ten science after the last two days. The grade tens were perfect today and I was able to lead them in a successful class discussion.

At the end of the day, I had hall duty. I had to keep an eye on the front hall for forty-five minutes. There was nowhere to sit. Every five minutes or so, someone would walk by, but they were too busy to stop and chat. I spent the time pacing back and forth and talking to the tropical fish that were busily swimming in their tank in the hallway.

Wednesday, Feb 14

Valentine's Day is an important day in the life of the school. Elementary students pass each other cards and have a party in the afternoon. Junior high students don't have a party but they often give each other cards and bring sweets to share. Some junior high schools have candy grams to raise money. Children will purchase candy grams and have them delivered to their friends. High schools will often have a red and white day where students who dress in red and white earn points for future rewards. They will also participate in the candy gram activity. There is, of course, a Valentine's dance at both junior and senior high levels.

On this particular Valentine's Day, I was teaching junior high. One student brought in some red and white candy which he shared at the beginning of class. Unfortunately, the box of candy was knocked to the floor and spilled. I insisted that all the candy be picked up before we started class. Wouldn't you know, a couple of active boys had picked up most of the candy. When I started the lesson, there were flying red and white gum balls. I had to stop the lesson to collect all the gum.

In the afternoon, candy grams were delivered. It was great that some of the students got one but I felt sorry for those who are not popular and didn't receive any. It must have been awkward for them. On this day, one girl got twelve candy grams—all from the same boy. Impressive—and a little embarrassing.

Thursday, Feb 15

Often, in new subdivisions, the population of children expands before the government has a chance to increase the number of classrooms. Some schools become so crowded that temporary portable classrooms have to be placed outside.

I was given a grade five class today that used a portable

classroom and I had to travel to and from the main school all day. This wouldn't have been a big problem if there weren't several centimetres of snow on the ground and a wind chill of -30° C. The portable classroom didn't have much insulation and was a little cool. I had to keep my boots on to keep my feet warm.

However, the grade fives had no problem with it. If they needed to go to the washroom, they had to go into the main building. I had to continually remind them to put on their coats and boots. They were quite content to run outside in sneakers and t-shirts. I have concluded that ten- and eleven-year-olds do not have enough sense to feel the cold.

Friday, Feb 16

As the proverb goes, one rotten apple will spoil the barrel. That proverb certainly applies to students. There are far more followers than leaders, but why do so many leaders tend to lead in the wrong direction? It only takes one or two in a class to start to cause problems and many of the others will follow.

At Mill Cove there were many problems today. Students spoke out and would not pay attention. They refused to do their work. This seemed to apply as a common thread throughout the day.

The highlight of the day came when Cathy said to Helen, "I'm going to kick your little white ass." What fun! I had to get the vice-principal to remove Cathy from the class before the bell. Otherwise there would have been a huge fight.

Monday, Feb 19

Although it seems unfair, when bullying occurs, it is sometimes necessary to separate the one being bullied from the bully for their own protection. I suppose it's like the government's witness protection program, but on a much smaller scale. Isolating the victim, however, can have severe consequences for that child. Not only has their self-esteem been lessened by the actions of the bully, but now the child is also separated from the support of his or her friends.

At lunch time, I was asked to stay with Karen in the classroom. Karen had been removed from the lunch room because someone was bullying her. She had to eat away from the other students. Why couldn't the bully be segregated? Why is it that the innocent party has to be parted from her friends for her own safety while the bully gets to stay? It does give Karen a chance to express her concerns to an adult. After all she has no one to talk to except the adult. This might help in her healing. To be fair, I didn't know the circumstances and the philosophy behind this action but to me it seemed unjust.

Tuesday, Feb 20

Teaching at a junior high located in an upper-class neighbourhood is far different than teaching in other areas. These types of schools are few and far between and there isn't much substitute work at these schools. The teachers don't get sick as often because there is far less stress. It was nice to see how the other ten percent live.

Today I had that treat at Rose Wood Junior High. The children were eager to learn, polite and respectful—not one problem in the bunch. I did have difficulty with the equipment though. I tried and tried to pull down a projection screen and couldn't. When I finally did get it down, with the advice of the students, I received a "two finger" clap. Was this a sarcastic clap or a quiet clap? I don't know but it was worth a good laugh with the children.

Wednesday, Feb 21

Students love learning about computers. It's "hands on" which means they are occupied most of the time. They enjoy the instant gratification of seeing their work on the screen. Even primary children like to play educational games where they instantly receive rewards when they are correct.

It's always a treat to teach at Parkview Junior. Added to the treat was the teaching of tech ed. The morning was spent helping the children build their web pages and doing PowerPoint presentations.

The afternoon was wood shop. Now, I know very little about wood shop. In my day, girls were not allowed to even go into the shop, let alone learn how to use the tools. Everything I learned about using tools, my father taught me. The teacher left a movie for the children to watch called *Extreme X*. It was about extreme sports and monster machines. I think that he hoped the class would be interested. They weren't. However, in spite of that, the students were good. They got plasticene from the back and started modelling with it while watching the movie.

Their resulting creations were excellent. Jarred must have been hungry. He created a fast food restaurant scene with a hamburger, fries, hot dog and a drink which he placed on a tray. Greg was really talented. He sculptured a truck with a bicycle in the back of the truck. Every little detail was shown. He will have a future in sculpture.

Thursday, Feb 22

We face many issues in our own lives. Because of this, we often think that others could not possibly understand the countless problems that stop us from being whom we really want to be. Our own self-centeredness blinds us to the multitude of troubles faced by others, preventing us from relating to those we meet in a meaningful way.

I was back at Quaker Grove today, teaching a grade one class. This was a difficult group that I had taught before. The class had several students with physical problems and who needed a special assistant. There was one student, Angela, who stood out, however. She was quite bad. She would accuse others of doing something wrong so she could get the pleasure of seeing them getting into trouble. "Shane said that I was a poopy-bum," is just one example of her attempts. Shane, of course, had said no such thing and was bewildered as to why Angela would say so.

Angela had gone into the woods, an out of bounds area, at lunch time and was caught by the lunch monitor. As the monitor took a fire cracker from her hand that she had found in the woods, she told the monitor that she didn't have it, a blatant lie.

In the afternoon, I called the children up to the front of the room to listen to a story. They sat in the spot assigned to them on a carpet. Unbeknownst to me, Angela had a gel pen in her hands and proceeded to colour on the carpet. When I noticed it, I asked her to give it to me but she refused. I'll put it in my backpack she said. To avoid a confrontation, I allowed her to do that. I didn't want to forcibly remove it from her.

Later in the afternoon the children were quietly working at their desks. Angela broke the silence by saying, "Nobody likes me."

No wonder, I thought but, of course, did not express. "Angela, I'm sure some people like you. Everyone has people who do not like them, but everyone has people who do like them. I'm sure your mother and father like you very much."

Angela seemed satisfied and went back to her work.

Later, I talked to the assistant. She told me that Angela's father had left before she was born and that her mother had left the family two years before. She didn't know who Angela was living with.

I felt terrible. No wonder Angela was spending so much time trying to get people to notice her.

Later in the day, as the children were preparing to go home, I noticed that Angela was in the classroom by herself. I went to her and gave her a hug and a kiss. She hugged me back with such ferocity that I was taken aback. I wondered how many other hugs she had received that day, probably none and probably none in the preceding days as well. I know that if I go back to that class again, Angela will be getting more than her share of hugs from me.

Friday, Feb 23

Most children love puzzles as much as I do. Often, when they have finished their work, I will give them a page from my puzzle book to work on while they are waiting for the rest of the class to finish. This encourages skills in problem solving as well as keeping them from causing disturbances.

Rose Wood has asked me to work again today and the classes were just as much fun as on Wednesday. When the class finished the lessons, I put some puzzles from my crossword book on the board. It didn't take them long to solve them. They were much quicker at it than I am.

I had outdoor duty and the weather was fairly nice for a change. The children brought balls into the play area and played basketball, football, and baseball. I have never seen a group of young teens cooperate in sports as this group did.

Monday, Feb 26

Children sometimes have difficulty controlling their emotions. Not only do they not understand the forces that cause them to react in a certain way, they also do not know how to stop those forces before they take control. Very often, children will find themselves in an altercation before they really know why. This is different from the planned fights and swarmings that, unfortunately, are becoming more and more common. In those cases, it is not the emotion of the moment but a need to feel powerful, in control or revenge. These are the emotions that are far more dangerous but the former can be extremely hazardous as well.

At Kennedy Drive, I was sitting in the classroom looking over the next lesson, when I heard a commotion in the hall. I immediately rushed out in the hall, only to see a boy being pushed into the glass window of the class across the way. There were several young men trying to stop the fight. When I arrived, one had grabbed one of them and was holding his arms so he couldn't retaliate. Others were just surveying the scene. I questioned the group and, to my relief, the guilty parties quickly owned up and went immediately to the office. No one was hurt and they accepted the consequences of their behaviour. The emotions that had led to the fight had dissipated as quickly as they had begun.

Tuesday, Feb 27

Having matches in junior high is of course forbidden. Because it is forbidden, it can be one of the rules that rebellious students like to break. This of course can lead to dangerous consequences.

At Ridge Road, the grade eights at the back of the room where becoming restless. I went to the back to see what the matter was and could smell the problem. I smelt smoke. Panic is not the answer, although some of the students were starting to get into that mode. All the desks had metal drawers so I knew that, wherever the fire was, it would have been enclosed. I immediately opened the windows and sent for an administrator who did an investigation to find the culprit. Apparently, it was not Graham who had brought the matches to school. Andy had brought the matches and, not willing to get in trouble himself, had asked others to set the fire. Graham, unfortunately, was the student who didn't want to say no to Andy and had lit the small fire. Graham received five days' suspension. As far as I know, Andy didn't receive any consequences for the incident.

Wednesday, Feb 28

Being a substitute means that, most of the time, the only skills that are used are that of crowd control and classroom management. A teacher has far more skill than that. After all, teachers do not get into the profession to control others. They become teachers because they love to work with kids and they feel they have knowledge and want to pass that on to others. Teacher training is all about teaching, not about controlling.

At Kennedy High I have been left a pre-calculus lesson to teach. *You mean I can actually teach a lesson today!* I excitedly exclaimed to myself when I found out.

I taught rational equations and had a great time. The grade twelves were extremely attentive. They knew why they were taking advanced math courses and were eager to learn everything. That is, all except one person, who still believed he was in junior high and had to cause a disturbance for the substitute's sake. Nevertheless, it was a marvellous way to end the month.

MARCH

Thursday, Mar 1

Some people are memorizers, others are problem solvers. At first, the learning of math is memorization. Children must memorize the order of the numbers. They progress to learning addition and subtraction facts. Then it's on to multiplication and division. Memorizers do well in elementary school. As they progress in mathematics, unless they learn to problem solve the memorizers fall behind. By high school most of the math is based on problem solving. Memorizing how to do one question will not help in doing another because the second question will probably need a totally different approach. I have sometimes been told by parents that a child who made A's in math in grade six is now making D's in grade nine. They seem puzzled, but the answer, more often than not, is that their child is a memorizer.

There is only two weeks to go until March break and I can hardly wait and neither, I'm sure, can the students. I was back at Dover High teaching math. Actually, I was not teaching, I was supervising. I spent all day watching students writing tests. Some of the students found the questions difficult and needed help with them. Although they knew the facts, rules and formulas, they didn't know how to use their knowledge to solve problems. Many children hate to be tested on problem solving because, in their experience, tests are simply a vehicle in which they can relate previously learned facts. Others find problem solving an exciting challenge.

Dwight finished his test early. He asked me if he could get something to do from his bag. I agreed, thinking that he would take out a book to read or some homework to do. No, Dwight did not take out these. Instead he took out his knitting. He told me he was knitting a scarf. I was pleased to see that there was no embarrassment on his part or, indeed, on the part of any other student in the class. We have come a long way in teaching our children that they should be doing what they enjoy regardless of gender typecasting. Dwight quietly knit until the test was finished.

Friday, Mar 2

True artists not only show their talent through their projects but also live their talent. Their creative skills extend to their personal lives and to their appearance. Their homes are genuine works of art. Creativity, in all areas of their existence, is essential.

At Dover High I was asked to teach art, political science and math. The math, of course, was no problem. Political science is OK because I like to keep up with the events of the day. But art? What a combination!

In art the students were doing visual puns, an intriguing project. Some of them had great imagination. There were drawings of a car pool, offspring, pork chop, bookworm and so on. I had never thought of the visual meaning of these words and phrases before.

Janet was especially talented. She not only was using her talent in her art class but she also used it in her appearance. She had braided her black hair and entwined it with neon yellow and neon green yarn. The contrast was effective and striking.

Monday, Mar 5

Unfortunately, there are dishonest people in all walks of life. This is especially true in schools. More children steal money and other valuables than adults because they have not fully developed their conscience and sense of self. To many of them, if it is left lying around, then it is theirs for the taking. Sometimes they will plan a robbery to obtain money to be used, especially, for drugs but usually it's a crime of opportunity. To that end, most teachers keep their classrooms locked if they are not there.

Today, I worked at one of the more difficult schools, Mill Cove, where I made the mistake of leaving my bag in the classroom when the door was unlocked. I did not have a key so I should have taken my valuables with me but I wasn't thinking. Twenty-five dollars was stolen. I should have known better, but it is hard to remember that some children just are not honest. I told the administration about the stolen money but was told that it was probably already spent in the cafeteria and that it would be very difficult to find the culprits. However, to my gratitude, they did reimburse me from petty cash.

The day improved when I received a compliment from Tammy in grade seven. "You are a very good math teacher," she said.

It is comments like this that makes it all worthwhile. I put these comments in a pocket of my brain and refer to them now and then when things get difficult.

Tuesday, Mar 6

I needed that comment today because the grade nine students at Ridge Road were bad…bad…bad. They would not give me a chance to say or do anything. All day long, it was talk…talk…talk.

In the afternoon, they were making bouncing balls with borax and glue. What a crazy but interesting chemistry assignment. I can understand why the regular teacher didn't want to teach it. By the end of the class there were balls bouncing everywhere! It was insane. *I am a good math teacher. I am a very good math teacher. I am a very...very...very...good math teacher.*

Wednesday, Mar 7

As a day-to-day substitute, there is little preparation work to do. Usually the teacher has already done the preparation. Sometimes I will mark assignments, but often the regular teacher likes to do that so she can see how well the students are doing and where their weaknesses are.

We woke up to freezing rain and school busses were pulled off the streets. When I arrived at school I was given a grade nine French immersion class. Most of the French immersion students were bussed in from various parts of the city so there were very few in class. In fact, in my home room, there were two students. In the second grade nine French immersion class there were four. We combined the two classes for a total of six students in one class.

Because of the combined classes, I taught only a total of two periods, as did my teaching partner. I informed the vice-principal that I had very little work but he didn't give me any more. I spent most of the day playing computer games and working on my puzzle book and I got paid!

Thursday, Mar 8

In secondary school, electronic equipment is forbidden. There should be no MP3s, no phones, no pagers, no iPods and no cameras. That doesn't mean that there aren't any but on the whole most students abide by the rules.

When a class was working at Kennedy High today, suddenly a pager went off. Before I could say anything about it, the guilty student had jumped out of his seat and rushed out the door without a word of warning. The rest of the class must have seen my astonished look.

"He's a volunteer firefighter," explained Terry. "When that pager goes off, he has to go to the fire."

Now I was worried. He was so young to be a firefighter. The firefighter didn't return, but I learned later that a teacher had had a chimney fire and the quick response of the firefighters had saved his home.

Friday, Mar 9

Sometimes the administrators are surprised by the skill of the substitute. Today, I know that the administrators were completely fooled by my extremely basic music knowledge. Perhaps I was fooled as well but, as the saying goes, you can fool some people some of the time.

I was asked to teach elementary band today. While travelling to work I remembered that I am the "world's best music teacher" so in I went. I had to go to two different schools during the day. The teacher actually went to three schools but one had an in-service for the day so that made my job much easier. The band classes were fun. They played tunes they knew and I let them express their music with gusto. I didn't reprimand them for not coming in on time or stop them when mistakes were made. Indeed, I couldn't.

Curtis, the percussionist, was especially enthusiastic. When the time came for his solo, he sped up the beat. This happened several times throughout one piece. I didn't want to stop them, but by the time they finished, my arm was aching from trying to keep pace. As I said previously, the only way I can keep time is to keep time with the drummer. At that point, the vice-principal dropped in and told the class that she couldn't believe that the band could play so well. I certainly cannot take credit for it. I had to thank Curtis, the drummer.

Monday, Mar 12

Teachers have many tricks in their classroom management arsenal. One of the most useful, to me, is THE LOOK. THE LOOK can express anything from amusement, to disgust to anger. It takes practice to perfect THE LOOK but when it is perfected it can be the ideal tool to prevent a student's misbehaviour without causing a disturbance.

I am back at high school today. Unfortunately, the teacher had left about fifteen to twenty minutes of work to cover the hour class. She, like all of us, was getting tired and desperately needed March break. Overall, the classes were great, and after they finished their work, they used the time to improve their social skills by chatting with each other.

Paul and Dan, two friends, were teasing each other. Unbeknownst to them, I was standing right behind them when they were calling each other "asshole." I said nothing at that point, turning conveniently deaf. Sometimes, being deaf prevents escalation of minor issues.

A few minutes later, Paul stood up and threw a wad of paper at Alice.

I became stern and said, "Paul, sit down!"

Paul complained.

To emphasise my command, I said, "Paul, also remember to be careful of the language you use."

Paul innocently said, "What do you mean?"

I didn't reply but gave him THE LOOK.

Paul mumbled, "Oh shit," blushed, sat down and said nothing for the rest of the class.

Tuesday, Mar 13

Goth is a subculture that has had a tendency to gravitate to the darker side of life. Although most teenagers do not understand the true nature of this culture, they do adopt the dress styles associated with it. In addition to wearing black clothes, they dye their hair jet black and wear black eye shadow, lipstick, and nail polish.

I am at Rose Wood teaching French immersion math and wondering if anything can be better than this. Pearl was a brilliant student who had adopted the Goth image. She had the black clothes, the black hair and make-up but she didn't stop there. She had drawn black streaks from the centre of her eyes and down her cheeks. She looked like a clown, but instead of bright colours, hers were black. Pearl, though, thought she looked great. No one else paid any attention to her. It must be a common occurrence.

Wednesday, Mar 14

There are many euphemisms used in school society. When the word challenging is used, you can be sure that the students who are so described are about the most difficult children with whom you will have to deal. Indeed they probably have so many personal issues that one who doesn't know these children will have a difficult time with them. In fact, a challenging child may already have had difficulties with the law and may be on his or her way to incarceration.

I knew the day would be difficult when the principal told me that the class I would be teaching at Mill Cove would be challenging. In layman's terms, this meant that they would be disrespectful, wouldn't sit in their seats, liked to wander the halls, wouldn't obey authority and wouldn't do their work. I was grateful that the problems I had today were not just mine alone.

In addition to the challenging classes, there were no

preparation periods and I had recess duty. That meant that I didn't have a chance to take a washroom break between 8:30 and 12:30. Not only that, to add to the problems of the day, I broke my glasses before coming to school and I couldn't read the instructions the teacher left.

By recess three students had been sent to the office and I had a major headache. The teacher had scheduled silent reading for the end of the day. With relief, I realized that was all I could manage. Indeed, that was probably why the teacher had scheduled it for that time.

Thursday, Mar 15

The law of averages states that everything eventually evens out to a common denominator. That is to say, that if you have a really bad experience, then you will soon have a really good episode which will equalize all incidents to reach the average.

There are two more days to go to March Break but this feels like the longest week I have ever put in. However I was back at high school, teaching grade twelve social studies with one half of the day as French immersion. The teacher had left exercises for them to do and there was enough to keep them busy for the entire period. Everyone in all the classes worked diligently. How much better could it get? Well, it got better. After lunch, I had a preparation period. Then the students left early so there could be team meetings. I was home by 2:30.

The law of averages applied as it always seems to do. If I have a really bad day then I can expect a really good day in the near future. Unfortunately, it also works the other way as well.

Friday, Mar 16

An important but understated part of teaching is to teach children to work as a team. After all, most of them will be expected to work as a team when they leave school. Often you hear I can't work with one person or another because of this or that. It is difficult to convince children to put their animosities aside and work together for the benefit of the whole group. However, teachers will do their best.

I was at Meadow Brook Junior High, teaching tech ed. and impatient, as were the students, for the day to be over. To be more specific, I was supervising tech ed. The classes were constructing bridges and know exactly what they were doing.

They were divided into groups. One student in the group was the supervisor, one was the manager, one was the supplier and one was the builder. They all had to work as a team to finish the project on or before schedule and at or under cost. Every supply they needed had to be bought with play money that they were given at the beginning of the project. If they ran out of play money before the project was over, then points would be deducted because of overruns. If the project was finished late, then points would also be deducted.

My job was to ensure they didn't take the supplies without buying them. It was a great day and I enjoyed it immensely but March Break will be better.

Monday, Mar 26

Hip-hop is a dance and music fad that is new to me. When watched on music videos, it looks so easy anyone can do it. Well, that's not true. It's a very difficult form of dance that required great physical stamina and skill. The moves are highly technical, and to be an expert, you cannot just flow with the music. You have to be able to do the moves slowly or quickly depending on the beat.

At Parkview Junior I spent the afternoon supervising hip-hop dance lessons. I decided to try to learn some moves with the kids.

The instructor was excellent. She taught each move in turn and then we slowly put it all together. She put on the music and I was lost. I shifted my right hip when I should have shifted left. I went forward instead of back. The students caught on but I looked like a whale in the throes of trying to escape from being beached. The beach won. After about fifteen minutes, I had decided that I had made a fool enough of myself and settled down to watch the kids. Besides, I was totally exhausted. After learning a few moves, the class had to improvise their own dance incorporating some of the moves. Some of them managed to be about as good as I was. Others were awesome.

Tuesday, Mar 27

Fire drills are an important part of every school. By law, there are a certain number of fire drills that must be carried out at every school. Sometimes the school is warned about a fire drill, sometimes only the teachers are told and sometimes it is a complete surprise to all of us. I always ensure that I know the fire drill procedures in every school I visit. You just never know when it will come in handy.

When I arrived, at Quaker Grove today, I was told I'd be in the library for two classes, and then I'd be given more instructions. Suddenly, a teacher went home sick and I was doing her class. Not surprisingly, things were rather disorganized. I don't know why, but the classes were rather abusive. I had to send about fifty percent of the students out of class because of their obnoxious language. However, the word got around and I had a great afternoon. That is until the fire drill.

Suddenly there was a buzzing noise and all the children stood up. I had not heard that type of fire alarm before but the children knew what it was. I grabbed the class register and followed the class out the door. Because I was substituting, I didn't know all the names of the children but I did a head count and all was in order, or so I thought. Then I was told by the administration that a student was missing. I took attendance and all seemed fine. I had the number I was supposed to have. But in actuality I did not. Jean was absent when I took attendance first thing in the afternoon. She arrived later when she was with another teacher. I didn't know that she had arrived. Jane had been pulled aside by the firefighters to pretend to be lost in the building. When I counted, I mistook the missing Jane for the absent Jean who was, in fact, not absent at all. No wonder I was mixed up. I apologized profusely to Jane for letting her burn up in the simulated fire.

Wednesday, Mar 28

When supervising tests, it is very important to watch that children do not cheat. Students are ingenious at finding ways to try to fool the teacher. Sometimes they will forget their calculator and ask if they can share a friend's. The friend will punch a math answer into the calculator before passing it on. There are the common methods of writing formulas on hands. Children will ask if they can listen to music while they work because it helps them concentrate. However, with today's technology, they can have answers rather than music on their iPods. Even cell phones can be used discretely. Text messages can be transmitted without a sound if the phone is placed on vibrator mode. Students can even take pictures of their answers with their cell phones and transmit the photo to a friend. One of the most common methods, however, is to write notes on paper and have it on the desk when the test is passed out.

Today I am supervising math tests at Sunnybrae. I spent the day watching the grade elevens writing the tests. Before the test, I ensured that there were no cell phones in the class and no earphones were visible. I made sure that everyone had their own calculators. This they were expecting and no one disobeyed the rules. Tammy asked me if she could have some scrap paper for the test. I agreed. As I was passing out the test, I checked everyone's scrap paper that they had on their desk. I caught five girls who had made notes for the test. I removed the notes and they had to write the test without them. They were not happy.

Thursday, Mar 29

Hip-hop is more than dance. Hip-hop devotees also wear heavy platinum and gold jewellery studded with as many diamonds as it is possible to wear. They call this jewellery "bling-bling." Now, I am aware that in junior high children don't usually have platinum and gold jewellery and most don't have diamonds so fake jewellery is acceptable among the teen set.

When I returned to Sherwood, I spoke to the teacher I was replacing for the day. She said they were typical grade eights and she was right. They were noisy and had no motivation. Luckily, I only had to send three to the office today.

Some of the children were eying the jewellery I wore. I had two gold chains that look nice when worn with a dark-coloured sweater. Josh and Abie asked if they could borrow them. I let them wear one each for the class, thinking that this might win the children over to my side. Josh stuck out his chest as he proudly said, "Now I'm bling-bling!"

Friday, Mar 30

Often children will surprise a teacher. When teaching junior high, I am not surprised by the disruptions and rudeness of the class. I am not surprised when I have to confiscate hats or iPod players. I am not surprised when I see them drawing a picture when they should be doing math questions. In short, I am never surprised at the rebelliousness of teens because that is their nature. It is all part of the natural biological impulse of pushing away parents and people who have authority over them and becoming adults in their own right.

French immersion is always a treat but today, at Nottingham Junior High, I was shocked at the students' behaviour. The principal told me, when I walked in, that the grade seven students would get down and clean the floor with their tongues if you asked them. I was sceptical but she was right.

From the moment the class started, they were completely engrossed in their work. They went over to the shelves and took the work they needed as soon as they entered the class. They opened their books and started working immediately. I didn't have to say anything to them. By the time I had recovered from my shock, they were totally engrossed in their assignments. The children didn't even look in my direction for most of the day. Some of them, I am sure, did not even realize that they had a different teacher. They spoke French to each other and to me all day, not because I was being strict about it but because they wanted to. Even Todd, who came from another class and asked for some cleaning supplies, asked for them in French. I wasn't needed except to be an adult presence in the room.

However, sometimes they were a little too helpful. I was trying to help Gisele and there were a few students trying to give advice. I said, "No comments from the peanut gallery."

The class looked confused and Paul said, "It must be a sixties thing." The others agreed.

I was really relaxed and thought I might get the class to take a little break. I started singing the Romper Room song "Bend, stretch, reach for the sky …" They looked at me as if I was from another planet. I suppose, in their eyes, I was.

APRIL

Monday, April 2

April Fool's Day is a day to be wary of when you are teaching. While senior elementary and junior high students have the most fun with April Fool, senior high classes are not above trying a practical joke or two. I always use the same April Fool's joke in class. At the beginning of class I inform the students to get ready for a pop quiz. Most of the cooperative students are not sure about it but will dutifully take out paper and pencil. The uncooperative ones will behave as usual and will be slow getting ready. When I announce it was an April Fool, the uncooperative students invariably say "You didn't fool me!" At least they are right once a year.

I was glad April Fool's Day fell on a Sunday this year so there were no tricks played but then I couldn't play mine. A couple of April Fool jokes from previous years are worth mentioning here.

Several years ago, I was given an apple on April 1. I wasn't sure about it but it looked OK. Before I was able to eat it, Steve felt guilty. He came up to me and told me to throw it out. He said he had poked small holes in it and had boiled it in fat. Deep fried apple sounded good but Steve was one of those boys who enjoyed practical jokes. I didn't quite trust him so I thought it best to follow his advice.

In another class, I was given a chocolate bar. Matt always had a little gift for me when I substituted so I wasn't surprised. I was surprised when I open the bar, though. Inside was a piece of wood exactly the same size as the chocolate bar would have been. He must have taken a lot of time to make the bar look like it had never been opened.

Tuesday, April 3

In high school, spirit is part of the atmosphere. It works in several ways, including the following. Firstly, students who are proud of their school will be less likely to cause problems and vandalism. Secondly, students who participate in school functions, sports and activities are recognized for achievements. Some of these students are not academically strong so they get acknowledged for their other talents. Thirdly, all the school has a chance to celebrate and have a little fun.

At Sunnybrae High there was a prep rally in the afternoon so all the classes were cut short to accommodate the rally. I was teaching a wonderful grade eleven class but I had to inform them that teachers were required to take home room attendance before the rally in case some of them chose to partake of other activities rather than go to the rally.

"How?" said Brian.

"Well," I teased, "you walk up the stairs, come into class and I take attendance."

Brian looked so angry that I started to laugh. "You must be from Cape Breton."

"No, Newfoundland."

"Oh, then you meant why."

Brian grinned and I gave him the explanation.

Wednesday, April 4

Plagiarism is a problem throughout the school system. Starting in senior elementary and continuing through graduate school, all teachers and professors must be on guard for any work that has been copied or bought. With the advent of the internet and the ease of cutting and pasting material into a report, it is sometimes difficult and time consuming to find out if material is imitated. Most high school teachers are aware of their students' abilities and a paper that is far above that ability can usually be recognized. Most junior high children lack the skills to hide their plagiarism and so can easily be caught.

During lunch at Parkview Junior, Mrs. Simmons was telling an anecdote about a student in grade nine who had done a presentation on a plagiarized poem. The poem he chose to claim as his own? "In Flanders Fields."

Thursday, April 5

For junior elementary students, Easter is about as exciting as Christmas. The lead up to Easter is shorter but the promise of an Easter egg hunt and many chocolate goodies leads to the excitement of anticipation. Parents get caught up in the spirit of the Easter season and like to provide goodies for an Easter party at school. A principal is not above contributing a treat or two.

Tomorrow is Good Friday and I am teaching a French immersion grade one class who are excited about the Easter Bunny. They are an extremely talkative group and were so energized that they couldn't stay in their seats. It occurred to me at one point that children should have seat belts at their desks. After all, it works well in cars.

Parents had brought in lots of treats for the children for the afternoon and the school provided chocolate bunny suckers. These were placed at the front of the room for all to see, adding to the excitement. After recess, the class had music. I had them hopping like bunnies to and from the music room, hoping that would make them tired. It didn't.

After music, we did language arts. The children were to work quietly on an exercise. I thought that it might be time to give them a treat. Perhaps something in their mouths might stop the talking for a little bit. I passed out the chocolate bunny suckers. Did you know that six- and seven-year-olds are good at talking with their mouths full?

The afternoon party gave me a headache but the children had fun. There were so many treats that all of them took a few home. I almost felt sorry for the parents who would have to deal with their offspring who were on a sugar high.

Tuesday, April 10

Sometimes the events that occur outside are so interesting that no one can concentrate on their work. The first snowfall in the autumn is a case in point. As soon as the first snowflake falls, someone is bound to say "It's snowing!" This causes the students to stop their work and start thinking about sledding, building a snowman or skiing, depending on the age. Some of the students will bound out of their seats to look out the window as if they had never seen snow before. Indeed, some of the exchange students have not, but they are in the minority. Reminding them that in a couple of months, they will be tired of all the snow usually gets them back on track.

For one class today at Rose Wood, I knew that I just couldn't compete with the events outside the classroom window and so I didn't try. The junior highs were watching a cop show play out in the street.

The sirens are usual in this area of the city as the school is located near a hospital. However, on this occasion, the siren stopped outside the school. That was the first sign that something was going down.

Sherry said, "Look, the cops have stopped someone." That was the end of my lesson. All eyes were on the scene outside.

They watched and nothing seemed to happen. The police officer didn't get out of his car. The car that was pulled over didn't move.

Suddenly, another police car pulled up behind the first. Now the class was really excited. The two police officers took the driver out of the car and then searched the car.

When lunch started, I warned the children to stay away. As she was leaving Sherry said, "WOW, I have never seen anything like that before!"

Wednesday, April 11

Anorexia and bulimia are severe diseases in our society. When senior elementary and junior high girls start to develop into women, they worry about their changing bodies. No longer are they the skinny stick-like figures of childhood. The influences of the actresses they see on television and the advertisements for diet program start them to wonder if they are getting fat. It is hard to overcome those influences and convince some of them that they are still growing. The weight they may be putting on at this time may be a signal that they are ready to start a growth spurt. They often do not recognize that the changes in their bodies are normal and that by the time they are eighteen or nineteen they will have become beautiful young ladies.

At Parkview Junior High today we had a speaker whose topic was anorexia and bulimia. The speaker was a woman who was about 5'4" and admitted that she weighed 86 lbs. She told the classes that she was dying because of the amount of abuse that she has given her body. She told the kids, in really graphic terms, about her gorging and binging sessions. She explained how she knew where every single-stall washroom was downtown so she could throw up if she ate anything. She told them about her laxative habit and how at one time she was taking over 100 laxatives a day! She explained that she couldn't eat anything now because her esophagus was so damaged that she couldn't swallow. She said that she was fed through a tube. At the end, she told them that, according to the doctors, she had about three years left to live. She was only thirty-two.

The classes were shocked, and traumatized at the same time. I know that the speaker wanted to help these children and I know she did. After the presentation was over, I resolved to eat sensibly and would never worry about that extra five or ten pounds again!

Thursday, Apr 12

Every spring and fall, bus students and their teachers have to learn how to evacuate a bus safely in case of an emergency. The procedure is as follows: the two students nearest the back open the emergency door and jump out. They then stand there and help everyone else get out. It is an important lesson to learn and I am sure that some lives have been saved because of the students' familiarization with the bus evacuation procedures.

For a change, it was a good day at Ridge Road. I hadn't been with this class for some time. Joan said when welcoming me, "It's Mrs. Claus!"

I had four good classes and one class was interrupted by a bus evacuation drill. I had to get on the bus and participate. I wasn't sure about jumping out the emergency door at the back but the bus driver, with a twinkle in his eye, insisted. I managed with the help of the young men who held me steady. I wasn't sure I could completely trust them, and had visions of them dropping me at a crucial moment, but they were great. The drill took one-half hour and it was a pleasant change.

Friday, Apr 13

Friday afternoon is always difficult when teaching. The children are anxious to be free for the weekend. Many children have activities all week and these combined with school and homework can leave them quite stressed. Two entire days without responsibility is a luxury for adults, but for children, those two days are essential to allow them to relax, play and otherwise maintain their innocence of childhood.

As I have mentioned earlier, the law of averages always seems to apply. Today was the opposite of yesterday. The junior high students at Mill Cove wouldn't sit down and wouldn't listen. They wouldn't do the assigned work. They had absolutely no interest in being in school.

By the last class, I had hardly any students. Most of them had decided to skip altogether because, after all, it's Friday and the teacher is a substitute. This often happens in high school, but in high school, the students are able to be in the cafeteria or the library with minor supervision. In junior high, supervision is usually essential.

All of a sudden, there was a commotion in the hallway. I opened the door and there were two girls in a fistfight. I got between them to stop the fight. Then I had to stop the few remaining students in my class from spilling into the hall to join in. Another teacher came along to quiet the situation down and helped to shoo the culprits to the office. I was glad when the final bell rang shortly thereafter.

Monday, Apr 16

Curious children are full of questions. From the earliest age one of their favourite words is "why." Why is the sky blue? Why does the rain fall? Why is my hair brown? Sometimes the questions children ask don't have an answer that they're able to understand but it's best to answer as accurately as possible. However, as the children get older, the questions get harder. Sometimes there is no answer to the questions.

I had an excellent grade eight class today who were studying cells. They had many questions about the topic. Some questions like "What's inside the cell?" I could answer. Others, because I am not a biologist, were not so easy.

"Do one-celled animals communicate?" What kind of question is this? Obviously, it's a well thought out and intelligent question but I certainly don't have the answer.

"I don't know," I replied. "Actually, I don't know if anyone knows the answer to that. Perhaps it's something you can research. The first step in the scientific process is to formulate a question. And that was a good question."

I did find an answer later, but I was only teaching that class for the one day so I couldn't tell the children. Apparently, one-celled organisms communicate with a type of signalling molecule that produces a chemical-communication system which is unique to each species. What that really means and how the communication system works, I don't know but still it's wonderful to work with kids who really want to learn.

Tuesday, Apr 17

Use of the laboratory facilities in a school is a special event for any class. It gives the children an opportunity to behave like "real" scientists. They learn to use the correct equipment and to use it safely. Most of the time, they are exceedingly careful in handling chemicals and doing the assigned experiments carefully.

Today I had the opportunity to take a class to the science lab. This is something that I normally would not do as a substitute because usually the junior highs are too immature to trust them with the glass beakers, water and Bunsen burners. Water is especially difficult. Children love to play with water and are not averse to starting a water fight.

On this day, the only problem occurred when it was time to clean up and they had to wash their equipment. One of the sinks became blocked. There was excess water. Guess what happened.

Wednesday, Apr. 18

One of the components of a family studies class in high school is teaching the students to become mothers or fathers for a week. At Dover High, the teens are given dolls that are programmed to behave like babies. Some of the dolls wake up and cry occasionally. The parent has to feed, change, burp or cuddle the doll until it stops crying. Other dolls are "difficult" babies. Nothing seems to soothe them. They will wake up in the middle of the night, screaming. The student has to soothe the baby doll as if it were a real child. All the students' actions are programmed into the doll and the data is downloaded so a mark can be given. Any neglect or abuse will cause the student to fail that particular segment of the course.

I am at Dover High today, for a change, teaching math. In the middle of one quiet math class, the doll woke up and started crying. Everyone started laughing and it was the end of the math work for the day. There were comments like "Shut that thing up," "Give him a swat," "He needs a father." They were having fun but I made sure that the kids were aware that these types of comments could be considered abusive. The "Mother" was highly embarrassed by the crying of her baby doll and eventually took it into the hall until it calmed down.

Thursday, Apr 19

Drug use has become a problem throughout all high schools. Principals and teachers try their best to stop trafficking and the consumption of drugs, but unless the culprit is actually caught in the act, very little can be done. One of the telltale signs of marijuana use, however, is the smell. It can linger on clothes and it is obvious that the child has been in contact with it. However, this does not necessarily mean that the child has inhaled. He or she may just have been in the presence of someone who has.

At Kennedy High, a student, Clyde, came up to me at the desk to ask me a question. He definitely had the distinct aroma of marijuana surrounding him. I said nothing to him at that time because, as most kids would do, he would probably deny any contact and I would have to prove that he had actually smoked it. Luckily, there was an assistant in the class at that time. I asked her to discretely smell Clyde to see if she could notice the odour. She confirmed my diagnosis so I sent him to the office.

Later the principal informed me that Clyde had unequivocally denied using marijuana, but he also smelt it and Clyde was sent home for the day.

Friday, Apr 20

Earth Day is a celebration in spring dedicated to the environmental health of the planet. Some schools mark Earth Day by cleaning up the grounds after a long winter. Others will put in a garden or plant a tree. Sometimes the school will make elaborate plans to teach their students about environmental awareness. Still others simply make an announcement over the public address system.

Parkview Junior had decided to celebrate Earth Day with environmental activities. The students were separated from their classes and put in various groups where they were sent to different areas to do an Earth Day project. Each project lasted about forty-five minutes. After the forty-five minutes, the groups switched. My group project was to make an illustrated poem about litter. The resulting compositions and drawings were excellent. I never ceased to be amazed at the talent displayed by young teens.

In the afternoon, we watched the movie *October Sky*. Although I had seen this movie several times, I never get tired of watching it. I find it very inspirational for junior high students.

Monday, Apr 23

The learning centre is one of my favourite places to teach. The children who attend the learning centre are so incredibly special. They are happy, cooperative and easy to get along with most of the time. Sometimes they become frustrated with the tasks they are expected to do and act out as most children will but after a short time out, they are back to their wonderful selves.

I had a great day in the learning centre of Parkview Junior High. My assignment for the day was Cheryl who was fifteen years old but had the mental age of seven. Cheryl was very cooperative and extremely cute. She loved to play games and so we did.

First, I read her a story, which she listened to intently. Then we did a little addition and subtraction. One of Cheryl's tasks for the day was to learn how to make a hamburger for dinner. We talked about the ingredients and then play acted about cutting up the onions (we cried), slicing the tomatoes, shaping the hamburger and so on. Later we went on the internet to research the prices for making the meal. I had a fun day and so did Cheryl.

Tuesday, Apr 24

French is a hard subject for me to teach but I do have a credit in French. However, social studies is my absolute worst subject.

It's a topic I am interested in but cannot do well. I failed most social studies classes in school but the teachers must have felt sorry for me. I made good marks in everything else so they gave me a minimum pass.

I am teaching at Ridge Road—core French and social studies. I am doing my best but getting rather frustrated at the behaviour of the students. Harry wouldn't stop talking. After speaking to Harry for the umpteenth time to stop, Harry looked up and asked, "Why are you picking on me today?"

I responded with THE LOOK. Harry cried, "Stop yelling at me!"

"I didn't say anything, Harry," I replied.

"Yes, but you look like you are yelling," returned Harry.

Wednesday, Apr 25

Phys. ed. is a subject I have avoided until now. I am not a physically active person. I have never been sports minded and my exercises of choice are swimming and walking. I hate playing anything that involves a ball that had a chance of hitting me on the head, or elsewhere on my body. I hate doing anything that requires me to run and maybe run into another person or have that person run into me. I don't like pain. However, I decided to try phys ed. today. There are very few children who think like me. Giving kids a chance to run around and kick a ball is their idea of fun. Phys. ed. is their favourite subject.

At Mill Cove, two classes are combined so there are approximately sixty children in the gym at one time. Because they are combined, there are two teachers, a male and a female. My job, after demonstrating the warm up, was to keep an eye on the girls and make sure they behaved. What an easy job. I had a great time. I only had to speak to one girl whose sweatshirt zipper had come down and too many of her natural attributes were exposed.

Thursday, Apr 26

It is a rare treat for me to teach at the adult school. To be able to relate to mature people is wonderful once in a while. For the most part they have great respect for the efforts of those who are trying to help them improve their situation in life. They come as failures. Many have had physical problems, others have been abused, and some have had brushes with the law. The older adults were in school before testing for dyslexia, ADD, or autism was done. They consider themselves stupid and unable to learn. Usually they are highly motivated and work much harder than their teenage counterparts. They have great respect for the knowledge of teachers and appreciate all the help they are given to improve their situation in life.

Today, though, I had one student who had no respect for his second chance at a high school diploma. Brian arrived in class almost an hour late. "Why are you late?" I asked.

"Slept in. I had to work late."

"Oh? Where do you work?" There was no answer to the question but I accepted that. His personal life was no business of mine and he probably had a family to support. I marked him late on the attendance sheet and gave him the sheets that he had missed.

He took them, put his head down on the desk and closed his eyes.

"Are you felling OK, Brian?" I questioned. There was no reply but he nodded before putting the earphones of his MP3 player into his ears.

Several times, as I walked around the classroom helping the other students, I encouraged him but he kept his head down on the desk.

About ten minutes before break, he started to perk up. He

lifted his head, took out a cigarette and waited until he could leave the class. He didn't seem sick or tired to me.

After break he came back in. He put his head down on the desk and repeated his previous behavior. "Are you sure you're OK?" I inquired.

"I'm fine. Just tired," was the reply.

He remained with his head on the desk for an hour. Then he got up, went to the back of the room and stretched out on a table. All the rest of the students completely ignored him.

When it was time to leave, Brian regained the energy that he had demonstrated before break and left the class.

So, why was he in class at all? What was his motivation to attend adult high school? Clearly he didn't want to graduate. And what was that job that kept him up all night? I have no answers to those questions but I can speculate. Often judges will give convicted felons probation if they attend school. There is nothing in the court order that says they have to do well. It is easier to do nothing in school than go to jail. And what about that night job? Could it be that he was a drug dealer or engaged in break and entry? I do not know the answers but it seems highly likely.

Friday, Apr 27

You know, it is strange how children can be so nice when you speak to them individually but can be very difficult to handle as a group. A class of excellent children can become THE CLASS FROM HELL if they are put together in the wrong combination. Junior high students easily succumb to peer pressure. No matter how many classes, assemblies and inspirational talks they have about being you and not following others, when they get together it's all about being cool. It's all about being part of the in crowd. It's all about peer pressure.

Today's class at Ridge Road was THE CLASS FROM HELL.

It was a grade nine class but their main concern, as a group, was to have as much fun as possible and to do as little work as possible. As a group, they did their best to drive the substitute out of the room. As a substitute, I drove some of them out of the room first.

Monday, April 30

Fighting in the halls is one thing. A fight in the classroom is another thing entirely. There are many objects in a classroom that can cause injury. The can hit their heads on their desks, chairs and tables. They can throw books and binders. Pens, pencils, rulers and scissors can be used as weapons. Innocent students can get in the way and some of them can get hurt. To protect children at all times, a fight in a classroom must, if possible, be stopped before it is started.

At Sherwood Junior High, Vince got out of his seat to put something in the garbage. Mauro said to Vince, "Don't throw that out; it can still be used."

Vince replied, "Mind your own business; I'll throw out what I want."

I could see that things were going to heat up so I went over to them. I tried to get Mauro to be quiet but he wouldn't. "Someone paid good money for that."

Vince, always quick to lose his temper, answered that with, "Fuck off."

I went to my desk to get a discipline form to send Vince to the office. As soon as I turned, Mauro, who had a history of fighting, had jumped out of his seat and struck Vince on the jaw. They started boxing in the aisle where students were seated on either side.

I jumped between, taking a punch to the chest that was meant for Mauro. The fight stopped. I knew that, by this time, Vince was calm. I held on to Mauro's shirt while he tried to get away. Finally he calmed enough so that I could talk to him. I asked him if he was OK to go to the office. He agreed, but when I went to release his shirt my fist was cramped so tightly I had difficulty opening it. When the adrenaline flows, I don't know my own strength. Both of the boys received three days suspension. I received kudos from the rest of the class.

MAY

Tuesday, May 1

Although many think the first sign of spring is the buds on the trees, I see the first sign of spring in children. Children are the first to dig out the bicycles, skateboards and scooters. When you see these, you know spring is here.

At Ridge Road, I was asked to teach grade nine science. The teacher was the head science teacher in the school and her classroom had access to the lab. It also had a sloping floor so that the students at the back of the room could see all the experiments that were being demonstrated at the front.

The class was working quietly. Suddenly I heard a noise. There was Brian, who had decided that he needed a little spring time fun. Brian, with a large grin, was riding his skateboard down the aisle. I confiscated the skateboard and took it to the office. Brian had to sit all day, wondering what kind of consequence the administration would be giving him. That was enough of a punishment. I had simply given the skateboard to the secretary to store for Brian.

Wednesday, May 2

The Alternate Learning Centre is for adults who didn't do well in the regular school system and failed or dropped out. Many of them are parents and have a reason to do well in school. They want to make a better life for themselves and their families. Today was my chance to see how the classes at the Adult Learning Centre were held.

Teaching adults, even if they are only in the late teens and early twenties, was much different from teaching children or even high school. There were no interruptions. There were intelligent questions. Homework was done. They appreciated the opportunity they were being given. They listened to the lesson, did the assignments and were so very polite. THIS WAS THE CLASS FROM HEAVEN.

Thursday, May 3

Immigration has been essential in the populating of Canada. Unless you belong to the First Nations family, you or your ancestors are immigrants. Because of this, and because of many exchange students from other lands, Kennedy High decided to celebrate the multi-cultural atmosphere of their student body.

The assembly started with students singing songs from their ancestral lands. There were dances and speeches. An exchange student from Austria gave a wonderful talk about the differences between school in his country and school in Austria. Then there was a parade of flags. Dressed in their native costumes, students came on to the stage one by one to model and wave their flag. There were students from various countries in Africa, Asia and South America. There were European students and those from Iraq and Lebanon. In all about thirty-five countries were represented. It made for quite a display on the stage. Finally, there were those whose ancestry was so jumbled that they could only call themselves Canadian. To a loud cheer, the Canadians came on stage waving the Maple Leaf. They modelled their native dress—hockey sweaters and sweat pants with ball caps!

Friday, May 4

Even the best of students try to rebel at times. The simplest occurrences can be an excuse to try to get away with something. A teacher, especially a substitute teacher, must be alert at all times for the tricks that children play. Many times the children win the small battles, but sometimes, it is the teacher who gets the upper hand.

At Dover High a polite grade ten class entered the classroom.

"Is that water in that bottle?" I asked Elaine who was carrying a half-full bottle of what looked like clear, flat soda or more unlikely water.

"Yes," she replied.

"If I took a drink, would I taste water?" I asked.

"You are not drinking my pop!" Elaine responded.

"Gotcha!" Elaine blushed and put the bottle away. It was a good day.

Monday, May 7

By springtime, the grade eight students are improving. They are finishing this part of the rebellious period of their lives. They are beginning to realize that soon they will be the seniors of the school. They are becoming more mature and more able to handle the hormone changes.

I am teaching grade eight poetry at Parkview Junior High and we were having fun. After recess, there was a contest to make a new Canadian mascot as the "beaver had died." Each class was given a garbage bag full of paper, ribbon, buttons, cardboard, balloons, and paper bags and so on. I divided the class into groups. One group made the body, another the head, another the arms and another the legs. By the time they finished they had a mascot that looked somewhat like a woman. They named it Ms. Barnstead in honour of their teacher. They said the mascot looked a little like her. The funny thing was that when I met Ms. Barnstead, I agreed with them.

Tuesday, May 8

Young teenagers enjoy assembly most of the time. They consider it an excuse to leave the academics behind for a little while, relax and perhaps be entertained. Since all assemblies are designed to give a message, the children are also supposed to learn as well but they don't see it like this. For them, it is an escape. Once in a while, an assembly doesn't quite work out the way it should and, although the children have fun, the teachers do not.

This afternoon at Parkview Junior, there was an assembly. This time it was a keyboard player and his son who was a dancer and singer. There was a major problem with the sound system. The students sat in the auditorium for almost an hour waiting for it to be fixed. It never was fixed and the guitar and keyboard could not be used. The dancer did a few moves to a CD. When he grabbed his crotch, the girls went into a screaming frenzy. This encouraged him and the move was repeated again and again. All I could think about was the prohibition on Elvis and his swivelling hips when I was their age. My, times have changed!

Wednesday, May 9

All elementary children have vivid imaginations. They will watch a TV show or a video and then think that it's reality. When they read a story, their imaginations make the story so interesting that they may stretch the truth. We have to be careful that when we are trying to teach facts to children that they don't confuse those facts with the thoughts that they have developed from watching years of cartoons. Children take much of what they see and hear literally. We, as parents and teachers, must be careful that all children are aware of the difference between fiction and reality.

A grade five resource student had read a story about whales and he disagreed with some of the information in the book.

Doug commented, "Whales are not the largest creatures."

"Yes, they are," I disagreed.

"No, the tyrannosaurus rex was as big as skyscrapers."

"They were smaller than that."

Doug measured about five centimetres with his fingers. "They were this much smaller."

I think Doug had been watching too many movies.

Thursday, May 10

I have changed my mind about phys ed. Phys ed. is easy to teach if the kids already know the games, but when children are new to playing cooperative games, it is not so easy. In grades primary, one and two the children need more direction from the teacher. Being a substitute teacher for the first time in this area, I was not aware of the limitations of the smallest students. I thought that if I threw out a ball, they would organize a game on their own and simply have fun. I was wrong.

I was trying to teach grade primary about movement. They were to go to different stations and do different actions with hula-hoops, skipping ropes, balls and so on. I gave up and we played Simon Says and Follow the Leader. The same scenario occurred with grade one.

Grade two was to play a ball game. I had a hard time showing them how to play the game. I thought they had played it before but apparently not. Several of them left the gym and I had to bring them back. I was glad when that class was over.

Grades three to six were much more comfortable with team games and I only had to give them the ball.

NOTE TO SELF: Don't take a lower elementary phys ed. job.

Friday, May 11

Every once in a while, I have a job that takes so little skill I feel that I have not worked at all. Although these days are highly enjoyable, if I had too many of them, I would be completely bored. This day was one of those days.

I spent the day teaching phys ed. at Parkview Junior. The most I had to say during the day was, "Time to put the equipment away. It's time to leave." My throat had a good rest and I was paid besides. Now, this is what I call teaching. I left knowing the law of averages would come into play and soon I would have a day that was a bad as this one was good.

Monday, May 14

Towards the end of the year, grade primaries have become school pros. After all, the year they have spent in school has taken one-fifth of their life. They know when it is story time, snack time, recess time and lunch time. They can get ready for home with little help. When a new teacher comes into the class, the love the primaries feel for their teacher does not change. They welcome the new person with as much enthusiasm as they would welcome their regular teacher.

Fortunately, I only had twelve primaries today because two were sick. Unfortunately, so was I. There was the usual helping with opening the granola bars and juice packs for snack time, the collecting of money for lunch and recess ice cream, the passing out of milk cartons, and the arguments about who ordered what but there were no disputes and no tears.

By the end of the day, I had a collection of pictures to take home drawn by the talented and not so talented. The "I Love You" on the pictures swelled my head and my heart and also cured my cold.

Tuesday, May 15

Cancer is a major problem in today's society. We must learn prevention at the earliest age to stop the progress of the disease. To this end, all high school students are exposed to the correct way to self-diagnose. I suppose I am from the old school, but when breasts and testicles are discussed with a group of teenagers of mixed sexes, I feel a little uncomfortable.

At Kennedy High I am teaching math and career & life management. In career & life management, there was a presentation on breast and testicular cancer prevention and detection put on by students from the nearby community college. The presenters made us feel at ease with discussions that were informative and educational. The students listened attentively, learning of the importance of prevention and early detection.

The final review was great fun. The college students had developed a mock game of *Jeopardy.*

"For one sucker, how often should you check for lumps in the breast?"

"For one gum, name a symptom of testicular cancer."

Wednesday, May 16

When students are learning work in which they are interested, they tend to be more motivated and work much harder. Discipline problems tend to disappear and the grades go up. Biology is an elective subject and the students who take it do so because they are interested. What a difference it makes.

All the biology classes at Kennedy High were excellent. One class was a little talkative, but after some of the classes I have had, being only a little talkative is a treat. There were only five students taking advanced biology. How wonderful it is to give knowledge to a group of people who soak it up as a dry sponge soaks up water.

Thursday, May 17

Working for the department head can be a little stressful. After all, he is the boss in charge of hiring and you want to do the best job you can so you'll be back. The flip side about working for a department head is that they have an extra preparation period so they can do the necessary administrative work. For me that meant an afternoon with no classes.

Of course, the department head also scheduled the classes so the drug dealers and addicts were nonexistent in his groups. Kevin, a good math student, was in high spirits during the day. After school, he sprayed me with a water pistol. The students surrounding him laughed and I took it in good fun. I wished I was young enough to chase him and give him what for!

Friday, May 18

Not having the time to prepare for a lesson can be stressful. I usually arrive in plenty of time to be ready for the day's classes but sometimes circumstances will prevent my best intentions from being fulfilled.

I only had an afternoon job to do at Ridge Road so it was nice to have a leisurely breakfast. I arrived at the school in plenty of time for the afternoon session. Unfortunately, the vice-principal was nowhere to be found. Neither was the principal.

When I found the secretary, she indicated that I was to wait in the staff room and the vice-principal would be there shortly. And so I waited. And I waited some more. The bell rang for the afternoon classes. Still there was no vice-principal. I went back to the secretary and she showed me to the classroom.

Everything seemed disorganized. At first, I couldn't find the lesson plan. When I finally located it, I discovered that I was to do a science demonstration that was described in the textbook. I couldn't find the textbook. At this point, the students were entering the class. When they saw me they immediately started to scribble on the board. I stopped them from doing this, found the textbook and started the lesson.

Demonstrating a science experiment without practising it first is a bit of an exercise in panic. I did my best, and it almost worked properly. I was actually amazed at myself for being able to do it. I repeated the experiment for the second class and realized what the results should have been.

The students were restless and talkative, but after all, it was a Friday afternoon before the Victoria Day holiday.

Tuesday, May 22

By the time grade nines reach the last two months of junior high, they are preparing themselves for high school. They have been the seniors of the school for a year and have, for the most part, been setting a good example for the younger students. They are excited, sad and nervous about leaving what has been their home for the past three years and entering into the unknown and hallowed halls of high school.

The students at Quaker Grove were no exception to this pattern. The group that I had on this day was making personal shields. In the example I showed them, I had placed the flags of my countries of origin. They used that example to research their own countries of origin. They borrowed atlases and encyclopaedias from the library to do research. It was wonderful to see kids doing such self-directed work with so much enthusiasm.

Wednesday, May 23

Sometimes the personality of a class depends on the personality of a teacher, especially after they have been in the class for almost a year. Today I was back at Dover High where the children greeted me with eagerness. Is it because they have a break from their regular schedule or is it because they genuinely liked to see me? It's probably the former but I choose to believe the latter.

I had two classes for one teacher in the morning and two for another in the afternoon. All classes were at the grade twelve level. The morning classes spent the time listening to my lessons and doing the assigned work. The teacher of the morning classes was strict but fair with her group and they responded to that.

The afternoon classes just had assigned work. They talked continuously and did very little of the assignment. I found it very noisy and hard to concentrate. The teacher of the afternoon class preferred to work with each child as an individual. When he was working with one person, the others would chat but they responded to him.

Both were successful teachers and most of their students went on to further studies in mathematics. The differing styles dictated the atmosphere of the class. Is one teacher better than the other? No, they teach in the way that they are comfortable and both do teach well.

Thursday, May 24

At this time of year, the calculus students are preparing to enter university to study science or engineering. They have dreams of becoming a doctor or perhaps the next Einstein. Teaching a class of graduating calculus students is a dream come true—except that I really have to work at the lessons because calculus is a subject that, if you don't practice every day, you quickly forget.

There were several boys in the class who were trying to solve a difficult problem after they finished their assigned work. They were doing it just for fun. Good for them!

Friday, May 25

The flip side of teaching a calculus class is that the kids are under a lot of pressure to succeed. Parents sometimes expect that their children can do more than they are capable of doing. Or perhaps, parents expect their children to choose a career that isn't really suitable for that person. One student, Peter, in particular seemed compelled to get a good mark.

Peter sat in the middle of a row, beside the blackboard. When writing a test, Peter kept looking around and twisting in his desk.

"Peter, keep facing front," I said.

"I have a stiff neck," said Peter. "I am exercising it."

Well, I wasn't fooled by Peter's explanation. He probably had a stiff brain and couldn't do the questions. I resolved to keep an eye on Peter. A few minutes later, he started turning his neck again.

"Peter, move to this seat in front," I stated in no uncertain terms. Peter didn't say anything. He meekly moved to the front seat, leaving his binder, books and papers on the floor by the board.

Peter did no more of the test. "Peter, are you having problems?" I inquired.

Peter looked at me and said, "I can't do it." He didn't put another mark on the test paper but he also didn't make another sound that class.

Monday, May 28

French immersion is another example of parents wanting more for their children than the children are capable of doing or are motivated to do. Sometimes a child will do poorly in a French immersion class, drop out the following year, and then find that he is behind everyone else in the English classes as well.

On this day, though, this wasn't the case. The grade nine French immersion classes were wonderful. What was even better is that, for three periods, they were combined with another class to watch a movie. This gave me some unexpected time off.

Tuesday, May 29

Field day in elementary is always an exciting adventure for the children. It's a time to celebrate spring, run, get exercise and win ribbons. Any change from the routine is equally welcomed by the teachers.

This morning I was teaching a grade six class. As always, in grade six, some of the boys tried to have some fun at the expense of the substitute. As always, this substitute had no trouble putting them in their place and the morning classes went well.

In the afternoon I was switched to a grade two-three class. This can be a difficult combination because the grade twos left one-half hour earlier than the grade threes. I didn't teach the grade twos, though, because of the field day.

The best races of the day, in my opinion, were the potato sack races. Watching the little ones trying to figure out how to get from one side of the field to the other in a potato sack was hilarious. They would hop and fall, run and fall, and trip and fall. Sometimes they would remove the potato sack and run, only to be told to go back and try again.

After the races, the grade twos had only enough time to copy down their homework and eat an ice cream treat. Most of them had to eat the ice cream treat quickly because they weren't allowed to eat them on the bus. The grade threes finished up a math sheet while eating their treat and then it was their turn to go home.

Wednesday, May 30

Family studies, in junior high, is a way for children to unwind and get away from the drudgery of math exercises and English reports. Family studies is only presented for three periods during a six-day cycle so it's a class that is eagerly anticipated. There are only about ten to fifteen kids in a family studies class. The rest have gone to another shop where they learn tech ed., drama or art depending on the talents of the staff and the availability of equipment.

In this school, one-half of the time in family studies is spent on sewing and the other is spent on cooking. The group I had this day at Mill Cove was doing cooking but instead of actually making cookies or pretzels or pizza they were studying health and safety in the kitchen.

Because they had to sit and listen to my lecture and do exercises, they were not happy. There was a lot of rebellious behaviour but most of the class did what they were asked to do. I'm sure the teacher, when she returned, heard many complaints about not actually cooking.

Thursday, May 31

Today I was teaching family studies again. This time, the teacher left instructions to bake gingerbread men. These classes were much happier. There was a group of three boys who could not take anything seriously. They should have been showing their cooking skills on the comedy channel.

"Did you get all the ingredients?"

"No, I thought you did."

"How much do you put in?"

"I don't know, just until it looks good."

"I'm not eating this!"

"This is really yucky, stir it some more."

"Did you add the sugar?"

"I don't know, did you?"

"I can't remember."

"I am not eating this!"

I spent the class listening to their banter and was thoroughly entertained. And, yes, they ate their gingerbread men.

JUNE

Friday, June 1

Sometimes it's good to listen to children and take their compliments at face value. On this particular day, the first day of the last month of the school year, a compliment is what I was given.

I was back at Dover High teaching grade eleven and twelve math. The classes were excellent because final exams are starting soon and they are anxious to do as much as possible to get a good mark. Exams are a great motivator.

"You are much more personable than our regular teacher," said Ethel.

Considering that I think their regular teacher is a particularly personable person, I was highly flattered.

Monday, June 4

Children often have the knack of making a person feel old, even when they are only middle aged. Anyone who has the least bit of grey hair must be at least eighty in the mind of a child. Thirty is considered ancient. After all, to a ten-year-old, it's three times more than their lifetime, a mind-boggling amount.

At a grade five class, I had the following conversation with Angela.

"You remind me of my aunt, she is really old."

"Thank you," I replied, perhaps with a little sarcasm.

"Oh, she is now," she said, "but when she was younger she looked like you. She's dying."

Now I really felt my age. "Is she sick?" I asked hoping concern was in my voice.

"Not as sick as my grandmother."

It was time to extricate myself from this conversation. "Angela, it's time to go outside and play until the bell rings."

"OK," she said and off she went with seemingly not a care in the world.

Tuesday, June 5

Hopping from one school to another can cause me to have flashbacks. It's often difficult to remember if I am teaching the inner city street-wise children or the protected children of countryside.

I was confused when Carter asked, "What is a four-letter synonym for *snatch*?"

All sorts of synonyms popped into my head, but I could repeat none of them in the classroom. Discretion being the better part of valour, I replied, "I don't know."

"Grab," said Angela.

"Of course," said I and Carter promptly wrote it in his notebook.

Did someone put him up to that question or was it said in all innocence?

Wednesday, June 6

Phys. ed. for elementary students, as well as junior high students, is a welcome break from the routine of the day. For elementary teachers, it's also a welcome break because it gives them time for preparation, marking and bathroom.

On this particular day, however, for me the break wasn't to be. The phys. ed. teacher was sick, and no substitute was available. Since it was a nice day, I decided to take the class outside for a game of soccer baseball.

In every class there are the athletes who try to be in control and the not so athletic who try to avoid being on anyone's team. Two of the athletes tried to convince me that they should be captains of the teams. Having had the experience of being the not-so-athletic student, I said no. It's very uncomfortable to be the last person chosen time and time again.

I numbered the students 'one' or 'two' and sent them to their teams. I then chose the student, who seemed to be the leader, to captain each team. When I looked around, I found a few students hiding behind the bushes. Obviously, they didn't want to play at all.

I ensured that every student had at least one chance at bat. The teammates were wonderful at encouraging the weaker players. They offered tips on how to kick the ball, how to pass the ball and so on. The tips were well received.

Piero was a chubby boy, who was not very athletic. Three times, Piero watched as the soccer ball went between his legs before he made a move to kick it. A few minutes after his strike out, I looked for Piero. He should have been sitting on the bench, but no, he was behind the bushes with a couple of not-so-athletic girls having a great conversation.

Thursday, June 7

Boys entering puberty sometimes get embarrassed when their voice is changing. Although they look forward to the deep voice of adulthood, the squeaks that sometimes occur at this time can be highly embarrassing for them. At other times, the changing voice means that they are leaving childhood behind and this can be a regretful experience. These mixed emotions added to the mix of other hormonal changes can be a cause of difficulty.

I was back at Mill Cove Consolidated where I encountered a voice problem. Gus seemed to have had an instant voice change. I don't mean the change from boyhood to manhood; I mean the change from manhood to falsetto. He seemed unable or unwilling to speak in a normal voice. It was extremely annoying and any amount of correction from me would not change his manner of speaking. However, a detention for Gus did. Immediately, his normal voice returned. What a relief.

Friday, June 8

On Friday, typical grade eights can be even more typical, especially when school is almost over for the year. Obviously, the students know all there is to know about running a classroom and a school. A substitute teacher whom they haven't seen before simply interrupts the routine and really doesn't know how things should run.

After the first five minutes of the day, three girls were cooling their heels in the office. They had been sitting close together and chatting. They would not stop when I asked so I decided it would be better to separate them so they could not chat.

"Dawne, please move to this seat," I said pointing to a desk across the room.

"Why should I?" was the reply.

"Dawne, move to this seat."

"No," said Dawne.

"Dawne, you have a choice, either move or go down to the office."

"I choose office," said Dawne. She got out of her seat and left.

I tried again. There were still two girls chatting.

"Donna, I'd like you to move to that desk," I said pointing to the same seat.

Donna stood up and said, "I choose office." She left.

Good, I thought, getting ready to write a report. There is only one left and she has no one to talk to. I was wrong.

Judy stood up. Apparently, she could not stay in a class without her friends. "I am going with my friends." She promptly left. The three girls would rather sit in the office and deal with the consequences than stay in class and learn—typical grade eight behaviour.

Later in the day, I had the same class. The girls were back and one of them had not learned her lesson. The class was working on a project and Dawne asked me if she could research hers on a computer.

"Sure," I said, "as long as you only use it for research."

Dawne, as most children her age, thought that grey hair means no computer sense and poor eyesight. What she didn't know is that my distance vision is better than normal and I can see what is on the computer from far away.

Dawne was in a chat site. I went over to her. "Dawne, shut down the program."

She refused so I took the mouse and shut it for her. I again sent her from class. She refused to leave so I had to contact the office.

Why would Dawne continue to cause problems? Being a nice Friday afternoon, I can only assume that she wanted the rest of the day off.

Monday, June 11

Eight- and nine-year-olds are motivated by the smallest things. At Quaker Grove, I was given a grade three class. Most of these children are good but there are some who are going through a tough time at home and bring their troubles to school. There were many discipline problems in this class.

I knew I'd have trouble when Josh said, "I'm going to the washroom." Brenda followed with, "I'm going to get a drink." They immediately left. They didn't wait for a word from me.

Thankfully, there was a behaviour specialist who was assigned to this class. She was there for the morning and was a great help to me. She knew the students and knew what worked with them. She backed me up when I told Josh, Brenda, and the rest of the class that they must ask permission to leave the class for any reason.

Joel refused to remove his hat, even though he knew that the school policy didn't allow the wearing of hats in the building. Joel accused Josh of writing on the walls of the washroom. Joel refused to do any work for the morning. Josh was proven innocent. Joel was suspended for the day.

None of the children had pencils to work with. I gave away all I had and so did the behaviour specialist. Unfortunately, the pencils were new and the pencil sharpener didn't work. It caused quite a commotion trying to find children who were willing to lend their pencil sharpeners.

When the recess bell rang, the children simply ran outside. They didn't wait to be dismissed. They didn't wait to line up. I resolved to change that for lunch.

After recess, I decided to read to the class to calm them down. That helped a lot. Most of these children don't have books at home and probably have never been read a bedtime story. The behaviour specialist brought in milk and cookies. For many of these children, it was likely the first meal of the day.

After lunch, I was on my own. I decided to try my own tricks. For the first one-half hour, it was silent reading class. I told them they could have a sticker if they read. After twenty minutes, I walked around and put stickers on their hands.

The next lesson was several worksheets on bugs. I told them they could have another sticker for each sheet they did. Luckily, I had bug stickers in my bag of tricks that I bring every day. They worked hard on the sheets.

When it was time to go home, they packed up quietly and lined up waiting for the bell. These kids worked for stickers.

Tuesday, June 12

Children need a break from the routine as much or more than adults. Junior highs, in particular, find that the day-to-day routine can be particularly tedious. At Ridge Road, it was decided that, to break up the monotony, and to raise money, occasionally there would be a hat day. For the sum of $0.50, children would receive permission to wear a hat for the day. Over the year, the hat creations became more and more artistic.

One class was exceptionally difficult. They started the day by making and throwing paper aeroplanes. I was able to stop the aeroplane fleet from continuing but that was about all I could do in the class. The students stayed in their seats but there was a lot of chatting. Once the paper aeroplanes stopped flying, the children started making paper hats. Their creations were highly imaginative and kept them occupied and quiet. Even though they didn't pay their $0.50 for the privilege, I allowed the children to wear the hats.

Wednesday, June 13

On certain days, many teachers attend professional development days. Since these are scheduled for individual subjects or individual grade levels, the school isn't closed and substitutes are brought in.

At one elementary school, there were four teachers out on professional development. I won the substitute lottery. I was given music and resource. This meant that I had no home room and during some of the day had only three or four children in the resource room.

The music class was watching *The Sound of Music*. They had learned some of the songs and were interested in seeing how the songs fit into the musical. The resource children were doing work on syllables. I started doing rap music to emphasize syllabication. They had never learned it that way. I hope they found it useful.

Thursday, June 14

During the year, students like to display their talents to others in the school. It's always fascinating to see talented individuals display their skills.

One elementary school left the talent show until the last two weeks of school. The students were gathered in the gym and performances were held. As I looked around, there were nervous children with music books, excited children with costumes and teachers who were glad to have a few minutes to relax and be entertained.

I had a very active grade four class. Before recess, they were squirming and had difficulty concentrating. When we went to the talent show, I found that about fifty percent of the performers were from my class. They were a talented group.

There were the usual singers who could barely be heard because they didn't know how to sing into the microphone. There were African drummers and dancers who had practised well and did a good job. There were gymnasts who tumbled on and off the stage. There were comedians who told jokes that I thought were new when I was in grade four. There were the pianists who played "Twinkle, Twinkle Little Star" and other like tunes.

Then there was Gerald. Gerald, from my class, was introduced as a pianist. Gerald walked onto the stage without any music. *Here we go*, I thought, *"Chop Sticks."* Gerald proceeded to play a Mozart sonata. He was far beyond the league of any of the other performers. The amazement on the other teachers' faces reflected mine.

Friday, June 15

The teachers at inner city schools do their best to give opportunities to their students that they would not otherwise have. Many grade nine students at Quaker Grove are exceptionally grateful for the adventures that they are provided.

About one half of this group had gone to a sea school where they learned woodworking and made a set of oars. They now had the opportunity to learn to use them. They were going on a field trip to a community on the ocean where they would be taught how to row. Their teacher was going with them so I was asked to teach the remaining students.

The remaining grade nines were combined into one class and we watched movies all day. After all, said their teacher, these kids also deserve a treat, even if they weren't able to attend the sea school.

Monday, June 18

This is the last week in which I will be working. Next week, the schools will be closed so the teachers can prepare marks. The last day, report card day will be only an hour and substitutes won't be needed.

I have a grade nine class at Parkview Junior today. One of the classes was a learning strategies group. These students have had some problems in the past and needed some guidance and direction.

I noticed Eva take a pair of scissors from the teacher's desk and put them in her pencil case. I asked her to return them. Eva showed no remorse. She laughed and put them back.

Later in the class, Eva asked me if I wanted a hug. With my permission she gave me a great hug. At the end of the class Eva asked if she could go to her locker early. I refused permission.

"Is it because I'm black?" she asked.

"Absolutely not!" I exclaimed.

"Is it because I'm black and beautiful?"

"Absolutely not! It's because you're beautiful that you can't go to your locker early."

Eva responded with a stunning smile.

Tuesday, June 19

Primaries don't like change and are sure to tell you when they think you are stepping over the line.

This class had twenty-four lively students. I went from one to another to help them with their assignments. They were reading little books that they had made. "This is an apple. It is red. This is a turtle. It is green." I don't think they were actually reading the words. They were reading the pictures. By recess I was exhausted.

After recess, Alexandra said to me, "You are here for only one day. Mrs. Edwards will be back tomorrow." She wanted to make sure I understood that I was only filling in.

Wednesday, June 20

Every once in a while, children surprise me. I was at Parkview Junior High for the day. During the morning announcements, the vice-principal said, "Settle your classes for the announcements."

I looked at the grade nine class I had and said, "Settle down." I laughed and I was the only one laughing although a few smiled. The children had come into class, sat in their correct seats and had said not a word. It was so silent that had I not seen them, I'd have thought I was in an empty classroom. They were like that all day. Some days I have a treat, and this was one.

Thursday, June 21
Seven- and eight-year-olds have a great imagination and are usually supportive of each other. This particular grade two class followed the model to a T. There were only seventeen of them and they were all wonderful friends. They had no shyness about sharing stories with me.

Holden showed me a gap in his mouth and said, "Here is a twonie I received from the tooth fairy."

Cautiously, I asked, "Did you see the tooth fairy?"

"Oh yes, I made sure I'd stay awake until 2:00 so I'd see her."

I knew I was treading on dangerous ground when I said, "I have never seen her. What does she look like?"

"She is about this high." Holden indicated a space of about 2 cm with his fingers.

Friday, June 22
The last full day of classes always causes some problems. Some children are nervous about grading. All the children are excited about summer vacation. The teachers are exhausted and looking forward to a good break.

For my final day, I had a grade eight class at Meadowbrook Junior High. They were finishing exercises and doing final tests. Everyone was working well. Suddenly I heard a loud bang. Darrell was face down on the floor. He was unconscious and his legs were twitching. The rest of the class was laughing. By the time I got things under control, Darrell had jumped up and was back in his seat. He seemed really dazed so I asked him to go to the office and call home. He refused. I sent a note to the office and

Darrell was removed by the guidance counsellor. He returned a half hour later and was quiet for the rest of the day.

Upon speaking to the other teachers, I was told that Darrell wasn't above doing something like that on purpose to cause a commotion. I really think that this was the real thing and was glad no one was hurt.

Saturday, June 23

It's Saturday and the start of my vacation. I have had a good year. I worked every day and enjoyed the laughter, the elation, the tears and the exhaustion. It's time for a much-needed rest before I begin again in September.